2/14/84

to

Muriel & Joseph
Best
Allan Fromme

60+
PLANNING IT,
LIVING IT,
LOVING IT

Books by Dr. Allan Fromme

SEX AND MARRIAGE

THE ABC OF CHILD CARE

THE ABILITY TO LOVE

UNDERSTANDING THE SEXUAL RESPONSE IN HUMANS

OUR TROUBLED SELVES

A WOMAN'S CRITICAL YEARS

THE BOOK FOR NORMAL NEUROTICS

60+: PLANNING IT, LIVING IT, LOVING IT

60 +

PLANNING IT,

LIVING IT,

LOVING IT

Allan Fromme, Ph.D.

Farrar, Straus & Giroux
NEW YORK

Parts of this book first appeared, in slightly different form,
in *50plus* magazine.

Library of Congress Cataloging in Publication Data

Fromme, Allan.
    60+ : planning it, living it, loving it.
        1. Aged—United States—Psychology.   2. Aged—
United States—Social conditions.   3. Marriage—United
States.   4. Family—United States   I. Title.   II. Title:
Sixty plus.
HQ1064.U5F76   1983   305.2'6'0973   83-18211

To Bert and her friends,
who have not allowed the years to diminish
their appetite for life

CONTENTS

Contents   ix

PREFACE

In such a stubbornly youth-oriented society as ours, it's easy to overlook the advantages of age. That very phrase raised eyebrows among the older people I confronted with it. Advantages of age? The answers were not quick in coming. Everyone spoke much more easily about how much better off he or she and the world were in the past.

It's true that age, which at first seems millennia away, eventually catches up to us—with some depressing effects. By thirty, we feel removed from the carefree days of our youth, totally immersed in adult life. Forty is interesting to many, foreshadowing a change of life that nowadays rarely occurs at this landmark. Fifty is a common breeding ground for depression. It's here that the feeling of age—old age—starts to become a reality. Bodily changes that took place over many years, ranging from an increase in girth to menopause—not to mention illness, operations, and failing vitality—gang up on us and leave us with a sense of being only a fraction of what we once were. We get used to this by sixty—not that it becomes any more pleasant. Retirement is imminent, an event felt by many to mean flatly, "Your services are no longer required."

What we feared would happen happens. We're dropped, let go, not needed. What are we going to do? How are we going to spend our time? We can't just fish and play golf. Are we going to have anything important to do? Soon we'll begin to feel alone. The phone won't ring. We'll hear about and see more cases of poor health and sickness than at any other period of our lives. Some of our friends and family members will die, leaving us not only with fewer companions but also with the grim reminder of our own mortality. How much longer will we go on? And how will we adjust to the sharp reduction in our income that retirement brings? Will our money last?

We have a sense of being separated from our previous active life by a thin veil of depression dully expressed in the feeling that there is no longer anything new or good to look forward to. Our value to others, as well as our own self-esteem, has eroded away. Laughter, sexual satisfaction, the exhilaration of meeting a challenge, the sense of well-being and involvement, all seem to be part of our yesterdays. Today and tomorrow have the character of some shapeless void. It's all very scary.

The above is a picture of the down side of growing old and, as such, accurately describes what happens to many people. A totally different picture, of equal authenticity, can be drawn to depict the lives of just as many other people who use their senior years not to mourn what they've lost but to welcome what they have *now*. The statistical fact is that we're healthier and more alive than people of our age in any previous period of history. Medical science has extended not only longevity but vigor as well. Psychologically, with few exceptions, we're all a lot more sure of ourselves than we were when we were younger. Experience has provided foresight into potential problems and ripened know-how into judgment and wisdom. But perhaps the most important thing we've gained is the gift of *time*—one of our most precious possessions! How carelessly, recklessly, we used to squander it. Then for years we were so busy we constantly complained about not having enough time in which to do the many things we desired. Age and retirement return that luxury to us. Essentially it's a gift of freedom.

When Thomas Jefferson suggested that, ideally, our form of government should be changed every twenty years, he might well have been talking about our style of life itself. By the time we reach our fifties and sixties, we're long overdue for a change. There's a lot we owe ourselves, and it's high time we turned our attention to the responsibility of improving the quality of our life. If we keep this in mind early enough, our life-style can be geared to provide this latter-day freedom. Maybe we'll leave behind our expertise in a given field when we retire, but we won't have to surrender our value to people. If we really open ourselves to them, we'll soon have more *friends* than before—not mere business acquaintances—and we'll have more time to do all the things we enjoy with them.

The decline in our energy and physical abilities needn't keep us from almost anything we'd like to do—even competitive sports. After all, heavyweight boxers don't fight lightweights; they don't even fight middleweights. Similarly, there's no reason for us to take on twenty-year-olds. If we play in our own class, there'll be even less to be ashamed of in our golf handicap.

The up side of age is as accessible as the down side. Both adaptations are equally valid. It all depends on our own psychology. We're easily influenced by our youth-oriented society to believe that youth is beautiful and age is something to be dreaded, to be cosmetically concealed. It's a pity we're so strongly affected by these superficial assumptions. A closer look reminds us that the people who spin the earth on its axis in world affairs and government, in business and administration, in show business, in virtually all areas, are people well on in years. Perhaps even more important than the fact that they have clout is that *they have fun*. Society's attention, more than we realize, is strongly diverted to the elderly who need care. We should also realize that there are many seniors who don't need care and are enjoying lives free of the pressures and irritations we all experienced for so much of our lives.

The magic of making 60+ the best time of life is in our heads. It's *how we look at it* and *what we do about it* that will make the difference between languishing and living. The sooner we refresh our outlooks, the better. We're all running late because of the way our youth and middle age absorbed us. But it will never be too soon to look at the opportunities age provides and to begin to use them to advantage.

I've been moved to write this book because I see all around me the needless despair, the unrewarding withdrawal, the sorrowful surrender of so many elderly people who are surrounded by unrecognized opportunities for the daily enrichment of their lives. Happiness is not simply a matter of chance; it most often comes from our ability to find and seize it.

There's a wonderful, if slightly irreverent, story about a priest whose church (along with most of the town) was flooded during a period of heavy rainstorms. The water was well up to his knees, and his congregation, of course, had stopped attending services. The priest countered all suggestions that he evacuate, referring serenely to his total, unfailing faith in the Lord. When the water reached his waist, people came for him in a boat, but again he insisted the Lord would save him. The water reached his shoulders. A helicopter was sent, from which a harness was lowered, bearing a note pleading that the priest leave the church. But he persisted in his unshakable faith that the Lord would save him. Finally, the water rose above his head and he drowned. In heaven, the priest requested an interview with the Lord. "How could you do this to me?" he asked the Lord. "I, the most faithful, the most persevering of all believers?" The Lord's response was simple and straightforward: "I sent you a boat, I sent you a helicopter. What more could I do?"

If only we had the wisdom to recognize our opportunities, I daresay we'd all be better able to save ourselves from being overwhelmed by life's difficulties. The purpose of this book is to help elicit some of the wisdom we all have but too often allow to lie dormant within us. This is a clarion call to "arise" and fight a revolution against decay in ourselves. It's the expression of an attitude, a credo, a conviction that after sixty life is more in our control than ever and that we can make it as full and enjoyable (even more so) as our earlier life.

Before getting into the text of the book, I'd like the reader to know how much it was improved by the editorial efforts of both Nancy Miller and Carol McKeown. I admire their splendid skills and deeply appreciate the devotion with which they used them.

My special thanks also go to Jess Gorkin for suggesting this project and for his continued interest in it.

Allan Fromme

NOW IS BETTER
THAN EVER

Most people have the notion that our growth continues for many years, then stops, and after some time starts again—in the opposite direction. Negative growth, or decline, is assumed to be inevitable. Is it any wonder that older people get depressed? They see only one way to go: down! And how can they believe otherwise in the face of fading powers, slowing reflexes, and illness, to mention only a few of the realities of age?

I'd like to describe an experiment done some years ago that has bearing on our subject. A number of the strongest players on a college football team were selected to imitate the movements and activities of some three-to-five-year-old children. All they had to do was copy what the children did—anything and everything they did all day long. You know what? None of them lasted! The healthy, young nineteen- and twenty-year-old football players were so exhausted after a few hours that they had to quit! They felt old, decrepit, and weary. But you and I know they weren't. Next to the children, they probably felt just as we feel compared to them. In other words, the way we feel about ourselves depends largely on the comparisons we make or the bases of judgment we set up. It's not at all the objective determination of fact people like to think it is.

Other common errors lie in our tendency toward self-aggrandizement. Ask a man about his golf game, for example.

"Oh, I shoot in the low eighties," he says, adding defensively, "that is, when I'm on my game." The fact is, he was "on his game" only three or four times in his life! Generous to himself, he confuses those few extraordinary performances with his average so that what he defines as "his game" is more correctly his ideal, not his generally disappointing score. You can't really blame him; blame the culture in which we live. We're all pressed to develop a level of aspiration without any relation to our abilities. "But you're overlooking the fact that I *did* drive a ball farther and was steadier in my short game when I was younger," many will protest. I don't doubt that at all. I'm sure you did play a better game, as I did. But can't you play an equally, perhaps even more, enjoyable one today? Our striving, demanding society makes performance and winning so important all our lives that many of us fail to learn the pleasure of playing. Our satisfaction depends exclusively on winning, thus defeating the very purpose of play.

We owe it to ourselves at any age to avoid allowing superficial social values to corrupt our better understanding. We drive ourselves enough at work; why should we carry that into our play? We all know we were more active and stronger when we were younger, but our success and lifestyle were not based exclusively on those attributes; our self-image didn't really depend on these traits.

"But I don't function mentally as well as I used to," the worriers remind me. "Sometimes I can't remember names or recent events." Do you know how many young people complain to me about the same thing? There's no denying the loss of brain cells as one ages, but we've got so many millions of them it doesn't really matter. What does sharpen or dull our memory are our habits of attention, which can be good or bad at any age. Just as the finest athlete gets soft and fat and slow when he stops caring, so do we feel as though age has impaired our memories, when what we've really done is become sloppy about how we listen to people.

Our rates of growth and learning are by no means constant. We triple our weight in the first year of life and at other times maintain the same weight for years. We learn more during our teens than we do during later periods which are regarded as our prime. But the fact is that, although our growth rates are predetermined, we're all eminently capable of learning more at any age than we do. When and how much we learn is more the result of what society expects of us than of our own potential. When society was involved in an industrial revolution, labor laws encouraged children to learn some skills earlier in life than they do now. Women are presently learning things they never did before, due to society's changing view of their potential.

It's a shame our society doesn't expect more from the elderly. If it did, they would be continually challenged and would see themselves as more able as a result. Young people's "kindness" in lessening their demands on their elders is at best a mixed blessing, particularly for those who implicitly define old age as a period of vegetation. These older people fail to realize that age is only one aspect or dimension of our being. After all, we can be old and happy or unhappy, healthy or unhealthy, active or inactive, vigorous or frail, and—most important of all—old and finished, or old and still learning and growing. A lazy, undirected young person can be duller and less productive, show less growth and learning, than someone fifty years his senior. Having lived less does not ensure youth. And having lived longer fails to establish old age. We should judge people by their life-styles, not by actuarial data for a driver's license or an insurance policy.

Of course, we cannot blame everything on society. Those 60+ers who change their lives by giving up their work or old life-styles are obliged to recognize the basic psychological principle that anything removed from a life must be replaced with something else. If it is not, we tend to fall apart. The first sign of this is the discovery of aches and pains and illnesses we may never have had before. We have made a change without the necessary growth to support it.

In short, being old means no longer growing. If tomorrow loses its meaning, monotony will rule and only decay can follow. Although we cannot help aging, we need not become old. We can continue to grow by learning, a process which constantly enriches us. It keeps our curiosity—a first cousin of innocence—alive. We continue to take delight in our discoveries, in the company of others, even in ourselves. We avoid boredom and keep the future bright. Although we remain mortal, our zest for life makes it good to the last drop.

 23

A Walk on the Beach

How often do we hear people speak of curtailing their activity as they get on in years? They see this slowdown not only as a reward for all the hard work that marked most of their lives but as right and proper, even healthier, as they age. The world will make fewer demands on them, they'll have more time for things, even for enjoying the luxury of just sitting and thinking for a change. It sounds ideal—on paper. The fact is, few of us can make the transition from a busy workaday world to this unreal never-never land without coming up with the psychological bends.

Take Henry R. His physician asked me to see him because he felt Henry's complaints had been getting "psychological" of late. He was suffering from aches and pains, but all his tests checked out negative and Dr. P. felt medication wasn't the answer.

Having just moved South, I hadn't yet opened my office. So I went to see Henry at his home, an attractive beachfront condominium. Henry was somewhat distressed because his wife hadn't yet left on her morning shopping trip and he wanted to talk to me in private.

I looked out at the sparkling blue water and the white talcum-powder sand and said: "How about a walk on the beach?" He seemed taken aback by the novel idea of an open-air psychological consultation but, after pondering a moment, said, "Why not?" We kicked off our shoes, rolled up our trousers, and off we went. The vastness of the area gave us as much privacy as a consulting room, and the informality dissolved the usual guardedness of a client's first hour with a psychologist.

Henry told me he'd never felt like this before. He'd always been known as a hard worker, extremely reliable, with one of the best attendance records on the job. "But now I couldn't hold a job for a day if I wanted one," he said. "I just can't seem to get started on anything."

I asked him what he had tried to get started on. What followed was a lot of circumlocution—words, excuses, reasons, all adding up to nothing. "What's more," he said, "the doctors take up so much of my time. My health has been just awful."

Henry, I could see, was well on his way to becoming a professional patient, at a heavy emotional and physical cost to himself. After all, you can't be a patient without symptoms. Of course, I didn't tell him this. We didn't yet know each other well enough for such brutal honesty. Instead, I got him to talk more about the job at which he'd worked for so many years with success and satisfaction. He'd made good money and was well respected; he'd helped and advised others.

Naturally, there had been irritants—nights he couldn't sleep because of the pressures of the job. "There were times I wanted to quit and become a beachcomber," he remarked and then, lapsing into his mood of hopelessness and futility, added, "But do you know what? I don't know how to be a beachcomber."

"Do you really want to be one?" I asked.

"Sure, if I knew how."

I shook my head in disbelief.

"I guess you don't think I could make it, either."

"Well, maybe as a part-time beachcomber, but I doubt

you'll ever become a pro at it. You see, I believe fish gotta swim and birds gotta fly. We are what we are, what we've been for years. In your case, that's a real advantage, not a disadvantage. You've been a doer all your life. Why should you give it up to become a beach bum? I don't think there'd be enough satisfaction in it for you."

"But I don't want to work the way I used to," Henry protested.

"No reason to. These are the best years of your life. Why should you go back to the drudgery and pressure of earning a living if you don't have to? You could live like a nineteenth-century English lord . . ."

"Listen," Henry interjected. "I'm not rich. I don't have to worry from week to week about my finances, but my circumstances are, well, moderate."

"But that's all you need unless you want to show off."

"Oh, no, I'm not that type. But things do cost a lot. Take travel, for example. Sure, I'd feel a lot better if I could spend the next several years traveling around the world. But I don't think I can afford it."

"But you probably *can* afford an occasional trip, can't you?" I asked.

"Yes, I can manage that all right."

"You've done some traveling, haven't you?"

"Yes, over the years. We made two brief trips to Europe, one or two out to the West Coast, and, I would say, a reasonable number of minor trips."

"I wonder how much mileage you got on those trips."

"What do you mean by that?" Henry wondered aloud.

"I suspect when you went to Europe it was a two-week package tour. You were probably so busy at work clearing the time for the trip that you didn't read a thing about it in advance. Nor are you enough of a photographer to have taken pictures good enough for you to live with and keep on display."

"How do you know that?" he asked, surprised.

"Well, I couldn't help but notice that the few photographs you had in the living room were exclusively of your children and, if you don't mind my saying so, not very good ones. You were too far away, trees were growing out of their heads— you want me to go on?"

"No, you're right. As a matter of fact, I did buy a fine camera some years ago, but I never seemed to have the time to learn how to use it properly. And you're right about the preparation for the trip, too. When I got on the plane I wasn't entirely certain which places we were going to visit."

"But now, of course, you have the time for all of that," I stressed. "There's a great deal of joy in learning the pleasures of anticipation, of reading extensively about the places you're going to visit. And if you learned to use your camera, it would make the trip itself more memorable."

"You're right," Henry admitted. "I think I would enjoy planning a trip. I like studying geography and economics. And I *would* like to use my camera more like a pro. I once saw an exhibition of close-up photography of flowers and I was fascinated. But wait a minute . . . are you telling me that the thing to do is not to learn how to relax but to learn how to do more?"

"That, sir, is the best way to relax," I replied. "Just being totally immobile is not relaxing; it's dying. Many of the things we do at work are actually good for us. They're sources of satisfaction. The trouble is, work is something we do on demand. It's something we have to do, rather than something we want to do. And we have to do *all* of it, not merely those interesting parts we happen to like. Also, we have to do it when it's expected of us, as opposed to when we feel like working at it. If you extracted these unpleasant elements from your work, you'd be left with a hobby. You see, retirement is not an invitation to inactivity. That would be just as bad as, if not worse than, overwork. But I know it's not an easy transition to make. We get so used to responding to pressure that without it we tend to do nothing at all. In short, it's much easier to learn how to work than to play."

"You know, what you're saying makes sense," Henry said thoughtfully. "I haven't done a thing this whole year other than be sick. I really could be having fun, and instead, my life is getting worse all the time. But where do I begin, how do I start?"

"Start with what you mentioned, travel-reading and photography. But you've got to be serious about it. You've got to treat each of these things almost like a job—a job you're doing for yourself. You're the manufacturer, the seller, and the consumer all rolled into one. You're going to get paid, not in money, but in the personal satisfaction of a job well done. Essentially you've gone to work again—only this time it's for yourself, and for the first time in your life it's going to have nothing to do with money. Activity, involvement, and satisfaction—these are the things you need now."

"Certainly you can't expect me to make a life out of reading travel books and doing some photography?" Henry asked.

"No, of course not. That's just the beginning. From now on, make it a point when you speak to people to find out what they do in their spare time. How do they spend Saturday and Sunday? You used to ask others what business they were in. Now is the time to find out what they do when they're *not* working. People who have strong avocational interests love to talk about them, and they're enthusiastic enough to have a contagious effect. Often they even invite others to share their hobbies with them. Take up every such invitation and give yourself a real chance to see if there's something there for you, too. That's the way to broaden your horizons and develop your inner resources."

"You think I can really make a life for myself this way?" Henry asked. "It sounds so trivial—like just fooling around. Is there really enough dignity for a person in a life like that?"

This attitude is the major stumbling block to enjoying life after retirement. Having been brought up in a society that emphasizes the work ethic, we easily lose sight of the fact that we've become addicted to work; we develop the idea that the only justification for our existence is the work we do—and how successful we are at it. But stop and think how many successful business or professional people you know whose personal lives are in shambles. A man can be a whiz at his job and still be a poor husband, a terrible father, not even a good friend. I don't object to the idea of being good at one's job—but it's not the whole of life. There are values other than work that are important in life.

Ideally, a man shouldn't wait until retirement to turn to these values. But once he has retired, he can pursue them more fully and freely than ever before. No longer does he have to prove himself on the job. Money and achievement need no longer dominate him. He has a new kind of wealth at his disposal—time. He doesn't have to restrict himself to those things that "pay off" or are "important." He can turn to a life full of good things, the things he's always wanted to do and enjoy, no matter how unimportant or insignificant they may seem. Only he's got to stop just thinking about that kind of life and start living it.

These are some of the things I told Henry R. I'm glad to say that he soon realized that when he'd retired he had given up a part of his life but had never replaced it with anything. He began to move around, spending more time with other people, talking about current activities and future plans. He saw the doctors less and his friends more. He hasn't got so much time now to worry about his aches and pains, and his life is a lot busier and brighter. He's learned one of the first great lessons of retirement—life is not what you *did*, it's what you're *doing*.

Practicing for Retirement

"Is there anything I can do *now* to prepare for retirement?" This is the question a friend recently raised at a pleasant, meditative lunch. Attracted to the warm beauty of the semitropical area he was visiting, he had begun to recapture thoughts of the good life normally crowded out by the race for achievement, success, money, status. "It's not that I'm not enjoying my work," he explained, "but I feel the pressure more. I'm more tired more often, and besides . . . you know I love sailing," he added with a twinkle in his eye.

The idea of *preparing* for retirement, of thinking ahead, planning, and, in fact, beginning to practice doing it in advance of the great change in life-style is the only intelligent approach. Most of us become so attached to our lot—whether we like it or not—that the idea of change is more often diluted into a mere dream. It becomes some never-never land, a graveyard of wishes never acted on. Generally, as Henry R.'s case illustrated, the most successful retirement is not the giving up of your life for another completely different one, but rather the surrendering of part of life (i.e., your occupation) for the fuller pursuit of those interests which engaged you only some, but not enough, of the time. We don't add new ingredients so much as we alter the recipe, and do a great deal more of what we used to do much less of the time.

What this means specifically is that if you look forward to reading certain great books after you quit working, the only way you can make sure you're not fooling yourself is to read more of them now. Notice I said *read*—not buy—more now. Of course you can start getting your library together, but you've got to make time to use it. The mere purchase of a sailboat or a vacation house doesn't guarantee its use and enjoyment. You've got to find the time, steal the time, to pursue and enjoy these interests enough to make them habitual and to leave you wanting more.

What interests you choose are an entirely personal matter. Your status no longer varies with them the way it did with the job you held. Being ordinary or expert is not going to affect your income. This can make life a lot easier, but inevitably one asks, as did Henry R., What does one do for status, esteem, a feeling of self-worth? Well, we can turn the tables and be smug and supercilious, sneering at all those successful high-and-mighty workaholics who don't see their own slavishness to a culture that allows them little more than the material rewards of their effort and achievement. (There are, after all, societies distant from our own that emphasize the value of such treasures as greater personal freedom, inner peace, tranquillity, quiet, love, and wisdom.) But such a judgment, even if valid in its way, is harsh and may smack of sour grapes. Having lived our life in a world where status and emulation, work and success, activity and effort have been conditions necessary for self-justification and social approval, how can we preserve our acceptance of self without them?

This is unquestionably the most difficult obstacle we face in planning for our vintage years. Even if we were to be accorded the honorable position of "elder statesman," the fact would remain that we are no longer in command. This "demotion" festers in us, breeding regrets and a sense of futility and helplessness. Additionally, we will earn less money—if any at all—in retirement, and no matter how comfortably off we may be, this bothers us more than a little. Worse yet, we perceive all these changes as marking the final phase of our life—no more planning, reaching, building. We feel as Thomas Gray must have in writing his "Elegy in a Country Church-yard": "And all that beauty, all that wealth e'er gave / Await alike the inevitable hour: / The paths of glory lead but to the grave."

From the psychological point of view, all these feelings are the consequences of a major error of judgment forced upon us by our society. In Nietzschean style, we are constantly taught to be "that which must ever surpass itself"—but not in the human qualities of mercy, compassion, love, humility, sensitivity, appreciation, helpfulness, thankfulness, etc. No, our goals are to get ahead, outdo others, win, be best, richest, feared and respected, recognized and treated as better than others. We have no schools to teach us to love or to get along with others. We do have business schools, along with a host of other graduate institutions to increase our occupational know-how. Our statues never commemorate great husbands, mothers, lovers—nice human beings—only military and governmental leaders.

Since we've been urged to believe this judgment of what makes life worthwhile, giving up our occupations makes us feel and look like we're quitting. And in a sense we are. Certainly we're relinquishing our power base in giving up our job. And in our society, "to quit" is one of the dirtiest verbs in the dictionary. But is it really? Isn't it true that often it is the coward who conforms, that many of the outstanding heroes of history were, in fact, people with enough courage to quit, to go their own way, to protest against the established order? Every major religious movement or revolution was started by a brave quitter.

Now is the time for your personal revolution! Before the

powers that be retire you, begin packing in your head and heart. Start now—do more of those things you dream of doing later. Open your mind to the freedom of being yourself. Granted, this isn't easy, because all your life you've been a doctor, lawyer, or Indian chief. Your self was the smallest part of you. Like most of us, you probably respond more to style and the current idols of the marketplace than to what you really like. Some of our behavior is more an expression of what is expected of us than of what we really feel. Let's practice being ourselves so when we quit working we won't feel we're living with a stranger. Next Saturday, have lunch before breakfast—just because you feel like it. Take that walk, boat ride, or bicycle trip you've promised yourself. Or, if you want to, go to one movie after another and eat popcorn until you feel queasy. It's worth it.

This is just to start you off, loosen you up. We know this isn't the way anyone can expect to go on enjoying life. The point of such a preliminary exercise is to shake loose from the cliché life has been and begin to rediscover your individuality. When you were on the job, you spent most of the time doing what you did best, but not necessarily what you enjoyed most. You knew how to sell well enough to make a handsome living and knew also that you couldn't duplicate that money by playing the piano in a cocktail lounge—even though you enjoyed playing the piano more than selling. Okay, now you have a chance to free yourself from your enslavement and do what you like best. You can now see that best is not best in all ways. What was best for earning money isn't necessarily best in terms of enjoyment.

It's this kind of change in values, in how we assess things, that should precede the major switch from what we were to what we hope to be. To approach retirement with the values and judgments we carried through life simply doesn't work.

We can give up the armor and weapons of the corporate battleground because there's no fight; we're no longer in a competitive arena where we have to prove ourselves. All we have to do is what we want to do. But that takes getting used to. That's why the time is NOW—before we're left feeling there's nothing more to do—to begin practicing for retirement.

Want to Relax? Use Your Imagination!

Most people see relaxation as a departure from work, pref-
erably in a horizontal or, at least, a sedentary position marked
by minimal activity. I've already touched on the radical idea
that learning to relax is really learning how to work. Let's
look more closely. Relaxation does not take full time. It's a
mistake to retire for it. There are many reasons to stop working, and the desire to spend more time relaxing may be one
of them. But this implies you've already learned how. If you
feel you haven't, you should start right now.

The first thing to learn about relaxation is that it must be
satisfying. Sitting and staring out at the ocean, lying on a
beach in the sun, doesn't mean you're relaxing—no matter
how healthy-looking a tan you get—if you don't enjoy doing
these things. Nobody rests by command, even if he's sitting
still. It's like what Hamlet said about sleep: ". . . perchance
to dream: ay, there's the rub." It's the thoughts we entertain
(or suffer) when we sleep or try to rest that make the difference
between relaxing and mere inactivity. The problem most of
us have is that although we can stop doing what we've been
doing for years, namely working, we can't stop thinking about
it! This can create more pressure internally than we felt when
we were working. We learn best to relax by *doing* things we
like with our time, rather than by merely collapsing into a
passive, inert state of inactivity.

But don't worry, relaxation is not all that strenuous, either.

Our lives offer countless opportunities for involvement, commitment, devotion to interests, causes, activities, but the mere *contemplation* of any of these can be relaxation enough. Take ten minutes to daydream. Play those three long holes over in your head and heart the way you'd like to have played them on the golf course last weekend. Or fantasize about the fish you played so expertly and caught, even though in fact you never had a bite. Relive that concert you loved the other night—without the help of your hi-fi set. Dream about how to push through that issue before the Town Planning Commission.

People object, "That's unrealistic!" Of course it is. But what's life without dreams and desires? We're not committing the crime against ourselves of mistaking the dream or wish for reality. We're merely luxuriating in our desires—not confusing them with our more realistic hopes and aspirations. So long as we know we're dreaming—no more, no less—it's a pleasant indulgence in possibilities, in ignoring the hard facts of life. As such, it has a restorative effect on us similar to sleep or rest. Such dreams are essentially a private, personal five- or ten-minute film in which the good guy wins and the bad guy loses. Needless to say, we can overdo it. But who spends all day at the movies or watching TV?

Once we recognize the fact that the secret of relaxation is in the satisfaction we allow ourselves, we can learn how to relax while we work. This is absolutely essential! The man who believes his work doesn't permit it, and insists that it's only after hours that he can relax, will never have enough hours left to make up for the physical and mental abuse he suffers. There are many small but helpful things we can try, if we are willing. One such innovation in our work behavior has been shown experimentally to be surefire. It is to stop for a break before or at the very first signs of fatigue. Small interruptions for rest, judiciously chosen, not only allay fatigue but maintain our mood and interest.

There are also ways to make work more interesting. Even someone who retires has things to do. The trick is to find out how to enjoy even routine tasks. Listen to music while repainting your garage. Play achievement games with yourself: see how much you can do in twenty minutes, stop to rest, and then try to break your record. It might be more fun to fix some of the things you've saved for a rainy day on a sunny day outdoors.

The point is that there really is no worthwhile substitute for imagination in the conduct of our lives. Without it, our habits remain implacable and the monotony of life breeds such boredom as to rob us of the fruits of rest and relaxation. Keep moving. Keep trying new ways. Ideally, play offers us the opportunity to use our imaginations. Work is an area that hungers for imagination also. The more we modify our work and learn to relax while doing it, the easier it becomes to relax when we want to relax.

Our Unrecognized Need for Change

No one is exempt from an occasional mood swing. Nothing is visibly wrong, and yet we don't feel right. We don't know whether we're sad or bored, tired or lazy, worried or restless. We sit and stew in our own juices, sometimes depressed, often agitated, trapped by our own inactivity. What can we do? If something comes to mind, we feel we've done it before; there's nothing new under the sun. There seems no way out. Yet, as mysteriously as these moods of melancholy and despair silently creep up on us, they slip away without observable cause.

Now, of course, there are many reasons why our moods fluctuate, ranging from "something we ate" to major trauma in our personal life. These are the things we're familiar with. What we overlook is *our deep-rooted psychological need for change*. This need has a physical side as well. Just sitting in a chair, however comfortable, we cross or uncross our legs, shift our weight to feel right. A good night's sleep requires periodic changes of posture because, being bilaterally symmetrical, we cannot rest all parts of our body in any one position. Just as our body suffers from sameness and inactivity, so does our mind. The very first law of attention is change. Even a priceless masterpiece on your wall goes unnoticed after a while. The advertisement that holds our attention the longest is an animated, ever-changing one. TV commands attention for the same reason: it's even hard to turn off a program we don't like because it constantly moves and changes, and we don't know what's coming next.

The less we respond to our environment, the more sluggish and inert we become. If we were less than human, we'd be as content as a cat or a dog to lie around in stuporous somnolence much of the time. But we get restless. We've got bigger brains than cats and dogs, and we respond to larger portions of the physical universe. When we unwittingly allow ourselves to slip into a life-style of narrow stasis, our distinctly human qualities begin to shrink. We talk less, our vocabulary gets smaller, our ties to human society weaken, and we get depressed or anxious. The benefits of our lofty position in the evolutionary scale are not without their price. Because of our greater ability to learn and adapt, we've got to *keep* learning and adapting. We cannot afford to retire surrounded by nothing but familiar items, people, and habits. That may seem pleasant and comfortable, but it's not ideal unless there are elements of change, novelty, discoveries introduced.

I do not mean to imply that we should jump to the opposite extreme and live such disordered lives that we never know what's coming next. That would be far too strenuous and do grave injustice to the thought that goes into making our environment comfortably familiar. It's just that, as we get on in years, we develop more routine in our day-to-day lives than is good for us. Must every breakfast start with the same juice or cereal? Must you really sit in that same chair every day to read your paper or watch TV? Must you take exactly the same walk, catch the same news program, shop in the same market? Justifying it all by saying that's how you like it and these choices are best does not lessen the cost of so much monotony in your life. Repetition makes you dependent on your choices and finicky about them, while at the same time you grow less tolerant of alternatives. Worse yet, a dullness inevitably settles on this routine, as it does on all routines. "Best" is often not nearly so good as "different."

It's remarkable how a trip, despite all its inconveniences, can freshen our point of view. A change in routine, a new scene, can help us become more alive again. But we really needn't go to the expense of travel to accomplish the same thing. There are almost always unfamiliar parts of town to explore, new foods, different news programs and papers to try, dozens of innovative ways to make tomorrow different. You can combine breakfast with lunch, skip dinner, watch the Late Show, and set a new record for how late you get up the next morning. You can make a long-distance call to that old friend you've been meaning to write, finally get down to the library to see what periodicals they stock, or find a seat in the back of the gym to watch the local basketball team practice. There are almost always night classes or lectures of interest, not to mention people who'd respond to your invitation to come on up for some coffee and cake.

A man I've known for some years attended a lecture I once gave on this very subject and reported several months later his own experience with shaking up routine. He told me that what I had said struck a responsive chord in him, and ever since he had been trying all sorts of different things. "I haven't made any major discoveries about myself—at least not yet— but I have to chuckle over how much less predictable I am to myself. I don't know what new things I'm going to do tomorrow or the next day. It's fun, I tell you, lots of fun. I guess you might say I just feel more alive."

This is what breaking a pattern by experimenting with oneself, trying something new, does for us. It heightens self-awareness by probing our own possibilities for satisfaction. It endows our tomorrows with a sense of adventure and excitement, keeping the frontiers of our life open. This is the essence of youth.

Many people give me a wary nod of agreement but then add, "It's too late. I'm too old. You ought to know you can't teach an old dog new tricks." Nonsense! We're not dogs. Our learning capacity even in senility is greater than that of a dog in his prime. Besides, these aren't new tricks. We've *all* been experimenting all our lives. It's just that we don't do enough of it. Even the most outstandingly fastidious, orderly, compulsive stick-in-the mud enjoys some occasional departures from his routine, if only as a result of circumstances he can't control. What I'm suggesting is that we try something new deliberately, voluntarily, instead of having it forced on us.

Starting the process is the hardest part, but a sense of humor can come to our rescue. "It's ridiculous, laughable, to think that I could do a painting. Why, I can't even draw a straight line," you might scoff. Good, then laugh at the ridiculous, laugh at yourself, and do a painting of wiggly lines. See how it feels. See how it comes out. See what you can learn by doing, trying, testing. The *a priori* approach (judging before experiencing) is as dangerous in life as it is in philosophy.

The point is, we've got to shake ourselves up and do more in the way of constantly reaching out beyond the perimeter of our habitual behavior. Not all of our experiments will be rewarding, but they'll save us from sinking into a rut. Activity—particularly new activity—projects attention from the self to the world outside. Even the irritants we may uncover will hurt less than our private aches and pains. Our efforts not only expand our relationships with others but rescue each tomorrow from being a dull carbon copy of yesterday. We feel most alive when we look forward to things. Making changes in our routine does exactly that for us. We may not feel a need for something different as acutely as we do our thirst, but change can be just as refreshing as a cold drink.

Live and Learn

On finishing a marvelous dinner at the home of some friends, I kidded the man of the family by saying he'd have to live to be 120 before he could possibly tire of such great cooking. His response was that his wife constantly came up with new dishes so that if he lived to be *twice* 120, he doubted he'd tire of her gourmet treats. She overheard our conversation and added, "I wouldn't consider myself a good cook if I were limited. Live and learn—that's my motto."

I was immediately struck with the relevance of that good advice, not just to cooking, but to life itself. Ordinarily when we come upon someone who does something totally contrary to our expectations and experience, we sagely comment, "Live and learn." But why wait for something surprising and unusual in someone's behavior to be reminded that learning should be part of living all the time! I have repeatedly pointed out the ill effects of routine in our lives—how it dulls sensitivity, perception, and attention, how boredom sets in, and how finally depression itself begins to shadow our existence. What better way is there of adding variety to life than through the learning process? We become more alive the less we live by rote and the more we invite the use of our higher faculties.

No doubt we all promised ourselves years ago that later on we'd look into many things we didn't have time for. What a monstrous rationalization that was! What we were really doing was developing the bad habit of putting things off, and we were busy enough to justify doing it. Now we no longer have that good reason, but we're stuck with the bad habit. We still feel "tired," although we have no reason to. Don't make the mistake of thinking that fatigue is an inevitable product of age. On the contrary, too many of the elderly do too little to get tired. They don't force themselves into activity, so they become bored. Then they interpret their boredom as fatigue and use it as an excuse for inactivity—a vicious circle!

The trick in escaping from this trap is to start living and learning at once—now!—even before you finish reading this book. "But start how? With what?" people ask. Half their question is an expression of resistance, a subtle way of saying, "I can't because I'm not sure I know what I want to learn (if I want to), and besides, I don't know how to go about it." Adult education is more available today than ever before. Go to the Yellow Pages, phone a college or several high schools, and ask what's available. Ask your friends about it. Then make sure you *try* something. Sit in on a lecture or classroom demonstration to see how you like it. Additionally, there are countless things to learn from the most available teacher in the world—yourself. You can easily obtain all sorts of instructional material and teach yourself. You can learn how to paint, sculpt, swim, speak a foreign language, dance, make jewelry, become an expert on the American Civil War, cook in a wok, make Greek food, study real estate, sailing, book binding, anything under the sun!

People in the retail business believe there's a customer for everything on the shelves. You, too, can find something or, more likely, *many* things to learn which will add to the quality of life. You'll feel more alive puzzling over the snags in the learning process, doping things out, improving your knowledge and skills. As we've seen, life is essentially a process of continual adjustment and growth. We can retire from a job, but not from life. Nothing in life is static; the process goes on. And so long as we encourage its progress, we continue to grow. The most rewarding attitude toward our vintage years is to see them as a period of new and increased growth. This is what we mean by "live and learn."

Retirement—Total, Partial, or Not at All

We're more interested in the quality of life nowadays than we've ever been. We may work as hard as ever, the pressures may be even greater, yet we treasure our weekends, holidays, and vacations. Many of us even talk fondly of the time when we might stop working altogether. Retirement is no longer a romantic dream fulfilled only by the windfall of a lucky sweepstakes ticket. It's a reality today, more available than it used to be, and given our interest in improving life, we owe ourselves a second look at the benefits and shortcomings of retirement.

The strong differences of opinion on the merits and disadvantages of total retirement suggest the advisability of considering some more moderate approaches. Even though the whole of anything is obviously more than any part of it, more is not always better. Sure, we often dream of the day we'll never have to look at the cluttered pile of unfinished business on our desk. But it's equally true that after giving it all up we often miss it and yearn to have a little of it back. It's a huge change in life-style, going from a daily 9-to-5 routine to freedom. Despite the rivers of blood that have historically flowed in the cause of freedom, we're generally less skillful in the use of it than we tend to believe. Retirement can be like an ordinary Sunday in the lives of working people: when we can do almost anything we want, we're not very clear about what we want to do.

The fact is, work is good for us. It demands activity, con-
centration, effort; it creates contest, drama, and keeps us in
constant relationships with people. These are all basic needs,
the satisfaction of which gives us a sense of being alive. This
feeling comes automatically with work. It's a component part
of it. Once we quit, it's gone. *We* have to create it.

So much for the pleasure of work. On the down side is the
"muchness" of it. We overdo it. The work ethic of our society
has misled us into believing that work is not only good for us
but ennobling—the harder we work, the more righteous we
feel. Even the pressures, irritations, and disappointments add
to our sense of self-righteousness. Most people are inevitably
influenced so strongly by this cultural pressure that even their
roles of spouse and parent, not to mention friend, citizen,
etc., are often surrendered to the demands of their occupation. These are the people who most often find retirement
disappointing. The phone doesn't ring often enough for them;
their activity level drops so low they get depressed; they're
not used to spending so much time at home with their spouse,
without business associates, even without pressure. Fishing,
golf, or walking on a beach aren't significant replacements for
them. Earlier they had promised themselves they'd read the
classics. They try, but find them slow-moving and dull. Such
people, except for those with some compelling medical reason, should not retire. They'd be happier at work and, at
best, should try for some reduction in their work load.

Most people find it difficult to burn all their bridges. For
this reason, partial retirement is an easier transition to make.
It gives us a chance gradually to learn to enjoy the activities
we think we'd like to pursue in total retirement. Desire itself
is fickle and unreliable; *acting* on our desires is the only way
to discover what we really want. Ideally, if all goes well in a
partial retirement, the work load we retained gets to be a

nuisance, standing in the way of the pleasures we've come to enjoy. Then and only then are we ready for total retirement.

Another way to ease into retirement is to do it piecemeal, assuming of course that one has such an option. Illness dismisses such a possibility, but even mandatory retirement, if a person thinks it through ahead of time, leaves room for part-time work. For example, as some people approach their final days in a large company they've been with for years they decide to explore a totally different field and take real-estate courses and licensing exams. Almost immediately on retirement, they slide smoothly into a part-time job compatible with their new leisure. This is only one of many examples of the choices people make to test their readiness for a complete change. Their desire to keep a finger in the pie exhibits a certain spunkiness: "I'm not ready to be put out to pasture yet." (Of course, we must recognize the danger of going to the other extreme and working as hard as we did before.)

We don't always have to rely on a form of employment to help us get used to retirement. We can decide to retire with more personal chores to do than we can handle. The idea is to clean up the odds and ends around us. There isn't anyone, no matter how thorough and efficient, whose life isn't surrounded by clutter. Some of it is even quite important: the changes we've been wanting to make in our will, the long-postponed re-examination of our insurance policies, our neglected coin or stamp collection, the people we've wanted to write to, the books we promised ourselves to read, the clothes we've wanted to weed out, the automotive-mechanics course we've wanted to take, not to mention just going through our drawers, desk, closets, etc. Tackling these tasks can be a full-time job for longer than we'd estimate. After a while, the process of slowing down, changing the rhythm of our activities, begins to take care of itself. It's the period of transition that makes the difference. Instead of an abrupt halt, which would really have all the impact of a crash, we make a graceful slide into another phase of life.

The point of all these suggestions is that the people who enjoy partial or total retirement the most are those who had created commitments and interests outside their jobs long before they quit working. Retirement doesn't leave these people floundering; it merely gives them more time to spend on interests they previously didn't have enough time for. You've got to retire *before* you retire—develop attachments and involvements with things other than your job. It's sort of like an extramarital affair, only it's not your spouse you're cheating on but your job. And you're really not cheating, either. You're developing legitimate parts of your life necessary to the improvement of its quality, and keeping your occupation within reasonable limits.

People differ from each other, rendering no one solution to the retirement question appropriate for everyone. "Seek and ye shall find" is an old bit of advice still relevant today. The important thing is to make sure that we seek. We tend all too often to fall unthinkingly into popular patterns of conduct that don't fit without the introduction of changes specific to each of us. The time to work on finding a personal 60+ life-style is NOW. Delay keeps us bound to where we are. Change keeps us alive and young. The answer you find must be yours alone, and you'll find it only by sampling as many alternatives as you can.

A Total Change of Residence?

There were times earlier in life when we all dreamed of recklessly abandoning our responsibilities and flying off to some South Sea island paradise. No one really believed in this fantasy, least of all ourselves, so there was no sadness in its unfulfillment. But there *is* something to mourn in our failure to take advantage of opportunities we have later in life—specifically, the freedom and wherewithal to move. It's then that we begin to realize how fixed we are in time and space, how compelling our attachments are, and how threatening novelty and change—even for the better—can be. It's hard to become adventurers if we've never been adventurous. Many settle for some excuse and remain where they are.

Those who do move would benefit from a few gentle reminders. The first comes from *The Rubáiyat of Omar Khayyám:*

> I sent my Soul through the Invisible,
> Some letter of that After-life to spell:
> And by and by my Soul return'd to me,
> And answered Myself am Heav'n and Hell.

In short, paradise is not the South Seas, the Sun Belt, or any other salubrious area. True, it can be easier to find happiness in oneself by living in a pleasant place, but it's *how* you live, the life-style you develop—not any special place—

on which your happiness hinges. If you just go somewhere and sit, you can be as miserable in the sunshine as you were in the cold. The change should be not merely one of address but one of commitment, involvement, activity level. For many this is easy because, no matter where they are, they find people, develop relationships, and throw themselves into things. There's no problem. They can stay where they are or change their residence and be happy because they already have the major ingredient of paradise within them.

What can we do if we're not members of this happy breed? Most important, if you're toying with the idea of moving, examine an area in terms of what you can *do* there. More sunshine and congenial temperatures are important only if you plan lots of outdoor activities such as swimming, boating, shelling, fishing, golf, or tennis. Many people move South to avoid Northern winters and spend as much time indoors as they did before. In such a case, what's the point of the move? On the face of it, not much . . . yet a person's inner desires may be emerging here. The appeal of those South Sea dreams probably lay not so much in the beach as in its symbolic freedom from responsibility. Perhaps a simple switch from the large city and a job to a small city and retirement could have satisfied this desire more exactly than running off to some hideaway in the Pacific.

Take the case of Mr. and Mrs. S., who did exactly that. When Mr. S. left his accounting firm, he and his wife agreed it was time to try what they'd always said would be the good life. They moved South to a small university town, rented a place within walking distance of the school, and obtained permission to sit in on classes. They took some together, others separately, worked harder than the registered students in some, and just skimmed the surface of others. They loved reading and attending lectures; they enjoyed the small town, the number of young people around them, their minimal dependence on an automobile, etc. They made friends and entertained young and old. In short, they had a wonderful time.

Although it's true that any place offers things to do, we tend not to give top priority to what is offered in a specific place when making our ultimate selection. Climate, cost, distance from friends and family, all seem to influence our decision more. But it's important to keep in mind that we're not merely planning a vacation when we consider a change of residence. We're not just going to lie in the sun for ten days—we're going to live in the new environment of our choice. This means having things to do that are more important to us than mere weekend activities. Ideally, there should be facilities and other people involved in our favorite pastimes. The best way to find out what's available is simply to sample such places. Try them out. Before you move, vacation in areas you are considering. Try to rent an apartment there for several weeks and pretend you are actually living in the new place. The whole exploration can be fun and, in the long-run, extremely rewarding. I know a couple who are having such a good time at this they consider it the best part of their retirement and have been at it for the last eight years! They've found the constant change more interesting than settling down.

It should be clear that the message here is: a change of residence should involve a change of life-style. If you're not looking for a change, your present home probably works best for you. Even a more beautiful place in a more pleasant climate wouldn't compensate for what you would have to give up by moving. If you do contemplate making a change, start with one in yourself. Only then can you choose wisely and pursue the good life in a new and comfortable area.

The Psychological Impact of Inflation

Inflation doesn't mean simply that things are expensive. It means they are *more* expensive, that we are spending more for things which used to cost less. And the older we are, the more painfully aware we are of this, and the more likely we are to be tied to a fixed income, which is undermined by rising prices. Young people are not nearly so alarmed by the cost of things because they've more or less grown up with constantly rising prices. That's all they know. Our own experience is different, and given our older basis for comparison, our shock is easily understandable. It's as though our children were using an arithmetic different from ours. Brought up in an inflationary era, they count by tens; we're still used to counting by one. For them, prices are tolerable; for us, they're outrageous, obscene, and threatening.

We've always expected to pay a high price for things of value, but inflation has increased the price of almost everything, regardless of its value. *Nothing* seems worth its cost anymore. Thus, not only are we threatened financially by inflation but we're also made to feel taken advantage of in virtually all our transactions. This undermines both our financial and our psychological sense of security.

Inflation can have an especially strong effect on men, because of the traditional difference between men and women in their orientations toward money. Having devoted most of their life to earning it, men know very well the work and effort, the risks and the limitations involved in *making* money. Up until fairly recently, women were absorbed in bringing up the children, running the household, and *spending* money to do all this. They were the ones who bought the food, bought the children's clothes, bought the cleaning articles, etc. They paid the going rate, whatever it was, because their attention was so strongly fixed on the need for these things that they had little alternative (aside from substitutions where possible) but to reconcile themselves to the price. Also, they shopped all the time, and as prices climbed by pennies, they noticed but were not alarmed by the escalation. A man typically went to the supermarket less often, so if he starts now, he will discover jumps rather than small but frequent increases in price. And jumps are, of course, harder to take.

In short, there are unyielding elements of reality in inflation which genuinely pressure us, threaten us, and make living comfortably a problem. But there are also psychological elements—equally real but less objective—which lie within us, not just in the outside situation. These psychological factors, added to the increased cost of living, can easily increase the emotional cost of our life. But by relying on our inner resources, we can rise to the demands of the situation and maintain the quality of living.

We need hardly be reminded that we live in a world saturated with commercial interests. Our wants and desires are constantly inflamed by appetizing displays of merchandise. Needs are even created out of nothing and then raised to fever-pitch. Like the hunt, which is even better sport than the kill, spending money is more fun, more exciting, than possession of the goods themselves. So compelling does the activity of the shopping center become that automatic satisfaction is taken for granted. Herein lies the attack on our values. Idols of the marketplace crowd out our ideals. Isn't it true that our homes are filled with clothes, gadgets, and assorted other items we rarely if ever use? Not to mention the things we do use because they're there but which offer no essential pleasure or satisfaction. We tend to focus so much on price that we easily forget it's the essential value of anything that should be the prime consideration. The only bargain lies in getting what we really want, what is good for us. Sure, a markedly reduced price grabs our attention and stokes our desire, but what is ownership going to do for us? After a little while, will it contribute to clutter, keep us from being able to afford other things we need more? Or will it bring such satisfaction that it would have been worth it at twice the original price?

We must remind ourselves that not all our desires and appetites are equally to be trusted. Our first consideration must be what we need to buy, not what we "need" to spend. Maybe we've thought too exclusively of making money and not enough of conserving it. We're finally beginning to learn how. Friends of mine have traded in their many-horse-powered automative monsters for economical, gas-saving compacts, which give them driving pleasures they never knew, while delighting them by being inexpensive to run. Others have sold their overly large homes and settled into smaller condominium apartments, which answer their present needs far more appropriately—and they can invest the difference, netting a handy return.

We can trim the costs of an enterprise as well as any efficiency expert if we change our orientation. "Less is more" is worth keeping in mind these days. We needn't deprive ourselves. Up to now we've all been overindulgent in our acquisitiveness. Look into almost anybody's attic and you'll see what I mean. As we rise to the challenge of living well with less, we'll begin to enjoy a sense of coping. We'll free ourselves from the fear of being engulfed by the economic forces around us. There are actually many people who are living better today than they did when the nation was more prosperous. Our personal condition need not be a reflection of the national one if we learn to deal positively with the psychological impact of inflation.

To Be 60 + and Needed!

One of the most precious things to be is needed—especially as we age. Not only do we enjoy the feeling of people needing and wanting us, but if they don't, we deteriorate. One of the greatest obstacles to the enjoyment of our vintage years is the absence of this aspect in our relationships with others.

My experience with 60+ers keeps establishing the truth of this again and again. A recent visit with some friends whose little grandchildren were present gave me a chance to chat with their old, arthritic nurse. I commented casually that it must be fun living with two adorable, if active, children. Her response was classic: "To be seventy and wanted, that's everything!" I pushed the matter a little further by reminding her of the many friends I knew she had. Once again, she put her finger on the heart of the matter: "Of course, but they don't need me the way these two boys and their mother do."

There's a rich, warm feeling of wholeness and importance in having people reach out to you. The fact is, we enjoy a good deal of this most of our working lives. Everyone from a janitor to a company executive performs a function society needs enough to pay for it. If illness prevents us from showing up on the job, we're missed. Despite all the discord and strife in the world—not to mention the growing alienation of people from each other in city life—we are still enormously interdependent and need one another for the products and services so dear to life. Unlike pioneers, we don't build our own home, fashion our own clothes, grow our own produce. Everything we do is for others—at a price, but nonetheless *for* others. Thus, we need others and come to feel needed ourselves.

Generally, we're not acutely aware of our interdependence until we stop working. The phone doesn't ring. We're no longer surrounded by people clawing at us for what they want. But soon we miss the very things we complained about. We resemble the overworked mother who for years looked forward to the time when her children could stand on their own feet—only to discover that once they're grown and gone she's no longer needed. The very core of her existence went with them, she discovers, and she feels hollow inside. The things she looked forward to doing with her freedom seem trivial and fail to give her an inner sense of stature or worth. Some people in similar situations report sadly, "There's nothing to get out of bed for anymore." It's as though they've lost their reason for living.

What can we do about this? We can't make ourselves needed overnight. Unless we're known to be experts on matters important to people's lives—like doctors, lawyers, financial wizards—what can we offer? Why would people need and want us? What good are we to them? That is the question which comes closest to the heart of the matter: What good have we been to people? It's the answer to this question that gives us an evaluation of the quality of our social and personal life. Not our *occupational* life, in which we were needed during the working day. It's what we did the rest of the time that counts now.

If we've been close to people, shared the joys and sorrows of our lives, we come to need and want each other. Mere physical proximity doesn't do it. Office workers within touching distance may never penetrate the psychological space between them. They come and go their own way and never integrate their lives. But when people learn to relax together, play together, talk to each other, and sharpen their mutual awareness of each other, the recognition and response they enjoy become addictive. They count on each other and miss each other when they're apart. In short, they need each other.

The lesson in this is that we need not offer a service ordinarily paid for; we should do things for each other casually, out of friendship, and with the same interest we would have in doing them for ourselves. The seventy-year-old nurse was right about the value of being wanted, but she didn't look far enough beyond the nursery to see that people come to need us, not only for nurturing, but also for companionship and compassion. It's easy to overlook the fact that we satisfy really deep-seated needs in our friendships. We tend to think of them as leisure-time activities of little consequence, but nothing could be further from the truth. Many a retiree makes the mistake of thinking he's unhappy because he's no longer working, when a more accurate diagnosis is that he made the mistake of neglecting to develop social skills and friendships in his early life. Being alone too much dilutes our sense of pleasure, distorts our perspective, and eventually leaves us feeling no one needs us.

To avoid this feeling, not only must we constantly make new friends but we must make sure we cultivate the friendships we already have. The easiest way is to make ourselves available. Many of us say no to invitations more than we realize—little ones like, "How about a cup of coffee, a stroll, or a movie tonight?" After a while, people stop asking us. We lubricate our automobile to keep it running properly, and we have to maintain our contact with people to make sure our relationships are running smoothly. Saying no doesn't help. The older we get, the more inclined we are to say no, and the less we should.

The most positive way we make ourselves needed is through the validity of our interest in others. People need and want this commitment from us. It cannot be bought. We become important to them in proportion to how much of ourselves we offer. Friends will seek us out, want to be with us, offer us respect and affection; we will have that important-at-any-age feeling of being needed.

KEEP YOUR MARRIAGE ALIVE— AND LIVELY!

The marriage relationship after sixty used to be seen as static: whatever was, was. Today, divorce and remarriage even after thirty years are becoming more and more common. Essentially this is testimony to our increased youth and vitality, not to mention the sanction society now accords to change in our personal lives at any age. We enjoy new opportunities later in our lives than ever before. Instead of a dull, hopeless reconciliation to the status quo, we are now free to move in new directions. This freedom brings not just the availability of alternatives like marriage and divorce but, more important, the responsibility of deciding how best to use them.

The fact is, marriages get better or worse—they never stay the same. I really believe this, and even though many people suffer because of these changes, in general our interests are best served by flexibility. The trick is to control it, to fathom our needs and move appropriately. Let's look at an illustration.

Donald B. retired a year ago and his wife regrets the day it happened. "He's with me almost all the time—when I'm cleaning, cooking, even at the supermarket. And he's constantly telling me how to do what I'm doing when he doesn't really know." Donald can't understand her complaints and believes he's being a good husband. What he fails to see is that being with his wife all the time is not a requirement of a good marriage. True, thirty-five years ago they dreamed

and talked romantically about spending all their time together. But that was thirty-five years ago. Meanwhile, they
learned to be happy with the partial separation imposed on
them by the obligation of the husband to go out to work. Now
Donald's constant presence annoys his wife and doesn't even
really satisfy him. The fact is, he's spoiling a good thing—
that is, his marriage—by overdoing it. His own needs aren't
even being met this way. Once he begins to act on them
more exactly, he'll recognize how *dependent* (as opposed to
loving) he's allowing himself to become.

This points up one of the gravest dangers married people
face, whether they're aware of it or not, as they get on in
years. Dependency! Of course if they've lived together up-
ward of twenty years, we expect them to be dependent on
each other, but when they require each other's presence
constantly, they are sapping their individual vitality. Soon
neither can make even trivial decisions without the other.
Their uncertainty robs them of their adventurousness. Interests and friends grow more scarce. Color and excitement
become things of the past. The dullness of their lives leaves
them exhausted, complaining, and ultimately in each other's
way.

Habits form easily, and it's often difficult to get back in
control of your individuality again. One of the great ways to
rescue or safeguard ourselves from dependency is to keep
our lives full of people. The virtue of maintaining a highly
active social life is that, aside from intrinsic pleasures, it helps
us maintain our objectivity about ourselves. By seeing others,
we keep our self-perception clear. With the give-and-take of
social intercourse we see another side of things, another point
of view, and keep our own thoughts fresh. When we eventually turn to ourselves and the person closest to us, we'll be
better able to see what we are doing to each other. With a

little luck, we might even see all over again what a good thing togetherness is. But so is individuality! Ideally we need both.

This is true in any period of married life. It's just that independence is automatically accepted earlier on and unthinkingly rejected later. Precisely because people do become more mutually dependent over the years, they need to work at maintaining separate elements in their lives. Each of them needs something different to contribute to their relationship. If husband and wife spend all day, every day, together, what can they tell each other about how they spent their time?

Their singularity is important in still another way. No matter how much people grow together, as a man and a woman each remains intrinsically different. The needs specific to these differences must be satisfied. Each partner should feel free to engage in traditionally "masculine" or "feminine" pursuits. Chances are these activities will put them in touch with others and allow them to develop a variety of relationships. The point is that, for all the value of intimacy, arm's-length relationships are good for us, too. Letting our hair down all the time can bring out the worst in us and make self-centeredness habitual.

Lest all this be misunderstood, I must hasten to add that although "less is more" in mature marriages—people can avoid overdependency and maintain a healthy and vital individuality—when this is taken to an extreme the relationship can be abused. A man, for example, who plays not eighteen but thirty-six holes of golf with his friends during the day and gin rummy with them almost every night has reduced the role of his wife to that of housemaid. Overdependency is bad for a couple, but it doesn't usually embitter anybody. Rejection does, and when a person, man or woman, feels neglected, he or she eventually feels angry enough to stop working at the relationship. This in turn has the effect of chasing the partner away, thus creating a vicious circle of ever-increasing neglect. No matter how well a couple may have adjusted to *not* being together because of his (and possibly her) work, it's reasonable for both to expect somewhat more time together later on in life.

A relationship is best nourished by avoiding extremes. The "great love" among people who are inseparable leaves me suspicious of overdependency, loss of individuality, and, eventually, of vigor itself. The "great freedom" of people who want to do their own thing often looks like an uncaring escape from their partner. Moderation is the best course to follow. Take a little, give a little. Everything doesn't have to be shared. It never was, so don't force it now. Share the important things—ideas, money, friends, the interests that excite you the most. Above all, act as though you care. The chances are you do—more than you know.

There's No Marriage like an Old Marriage

Most of our emphasis in life is placed on discovering, creating, developing, achieving—in short, *reaching* for what we want. Much less effort goes into holding on to it. We often come to take for granted something we wanted and strove for with all our heart and mind. It isn't that we've completely lost interest in what we worked so hard for, but that now that we have it, it no longer commands our attention in the same way. Maintenance doesn't excite us the way design and development do. More energy goes into dreams of owning a new model than into keeping it in splendid shape once we have it. We haven't developed the art of maintenance to nearly the same degree as that of achievement. This is true even of our careers, of which many have said, "It's easier to get to the top than to stay there." Marriage is an especially interesting case in point.

Virtually everyone in our romantic society marries with a sense of achievement. There's freedom of choice, a sense of good fortune in the discovery of the person who represents this choice, and a feeling of well-being for having reached a mutual decision. Marriage is truly a big event in the life of an individual. But we all know marriages don't last anymore (not that they were any better when they did). Do we choose poorly? Or is it that we're much better at finding and creating a relationship than at maintaining a marriage? Maybe we're not skilled at making something of the opportunities marriage provides for creating an enduring, fulfilling relationship? It's fairly clear that we're better at getting married than staying married. And it's no wonder when we realize that we enjoy falling in love and getting married more than staying in love and remaining married. Even our literature supports this. It's almost all about falling in love, not being in love. Premarital problems are handled romantically; marital problems, clinically.

Does it really matter? Does a marriage have to last forever to be good? What's wrong if it lasts only as long as it's good? Don't we often wish we could do certain things over? These questions, often raised quite seriously, are pointed ones indeed, all of which cannot—unless one is morally biased—be easily answered. But surely it matters whether marriage lasts or not. Rarely is the decision to divorce reached simultaneously; someone is usually hurt. Although children may make the adjustment more easily today because divorce has become commonplace, there is still quite a bit of difficulty for them, too. Moreover, subsequent marital ventures aren't necessarily improvements if the ability to maintain a relationship isn't improved. Unless people learn how to live together, love is fleeting and marriage dull. What was achieved by getting married is not constantly being renewed, polished, maintained. The early thrills and excitement of romance never remain as they were. They can erode into colorless memories or grow into substantial feelings of oneness, sharing, understanding, respect, care—all of which increase a couple's desire for each other.

The reason so many marriages do not sustain the love they started with is that people unwittingly expect to go on living as they always have, except that a spouse will be present. Such an arrangement is *not* living together, except in the most superficial sense. Sharing a roof over one's head or even the same bed isn't enough to keep people close, and certainly not enough to bring them closer. There must be constant sharing of thought and feeling with mutual respect. Only a long growth process can achieve this deeper kind of harmony. To remain lovers people must not only grow—they must grow together. Their initial strong feelings of love carry no enduring guarantee. They said and felt that they'd do anything for each other, but have they? The other areas of their life—job, friends, athletic interests, etc.—preoccupy them as they did before marriage and can soon take over. Unless love and marriage are given top priority and the rest of life is modified to support them, they fade.

Those people who do weave a pattern with the love relationship as its center need not suffer any lack of achievement in the world outside. A woman need not actively participate in every part of her husband's life to feel, and be, included, and the same is true for a man. With this kind of give-and-take relationship as its basis, a marriage can go on and on. And it will get better and better, proving that "there's no marriage like an old marriage."

Have You Become Too Dependent on Your Husband?

Many women confronted by this question rise up in indignation and quickly assert the very opposite, namely, that their husbands would wind up wearing two unmatched socks if not for them. This may well be true; any close or long-standing relationship is bound to develop *interdependencies*, and husbands *are* dependent on their wives in many ways. But who will fare better in the absence of the other? This is the ultimate consideration and it should give women pause.

Historically, man has been given the role of breadwinner, and even though this is changing rapidly at long last, most women now over sixty were simply never taught the skills necessary to earn a living. They are inevitably reduced to a state of economic dependency, with more ramifications than we have space here to cover. But at least one deserves our attention. Not having been close to the process of making money, women were also discouraged from learning about the management of money. True, they handle household expenses and perhaps a small savings account, but if they inherit enough to live on as widows, they are often unprepared to move about in the world of investment. Certainly it is not in the best interest of women to be uninformed in such an important area until the last minute. Unfortunately, many a well-intentioned husband still contributes to his wife's financial dependency by failing to share either his knowledge or his means. He justifies his behavior by saying she wouldn't understand, but overlooks the fact that he has never tried very hard to explain.

But a woman is guilty of becoming overdependent if she lets the case rest there. She needn't learn from her husband. If she wanted to learn how to drive an automobile or to play bridge, it would be better *not* to turn to him as her teacher. He'd be far less patient than a pro. There are courses available through which a woman can get to know more than her husband about stocks and bonds, money markets, automobiles and their maintenance, household repairs, gardening techniques, etc. Although it's easy to say, "Let John do it," the trouble is that too often he doesn't. Worse yet, if he does, the woman will feel no need to develop her own know-how— the only way to become self-sufficient and independent.

We understand from earlier in this chapter that the nourishing togetherness of a good marriage need not erase the separateness necessary for individual growth. It's healthy for women to realize that the more they develop their own potential, the better they'll feel about themselves. The growth of their inner resources will leave them with more to give. It's one thing to bathe in the warmth of a relationship; it's another to drown in it. A woman's social life is a case in point. If she's married to a man whose work involves him with many interesting and exciting people, she's swept up by this and neglects to make friends of her own. In such cases, the death of her husband will steal from her not only his companionship but, before long, her social world as well.

Just as a man has a life of his own in his work, so does a woman need a life of her own. Their home simply isn't enough, because it's not populated with people, as is a business. More and more women today return to work once they're free of their children. But even if they don't, they must allow their interests greater play, not only for the purpose of developing greater skills and enjoying them more, but for the personal relationships which will grow out of them. As we've discussed, a good marriage does not demand that everything be shared. As a matter of fact, the relationship is often enriched by the differences in experience husband and wife can report to each other. They can love each other, support and depend on each other, and yet stand alone or with others on many things. Because of a man's absorption in his work, he is usually far ahead of a woman in the duality of being independent and dependent at the same time. Women need encouragement to catch up, and they have to find ways to get their husbands to sponsor them in a healthy life-style.

A word of caution must be issued to those who challenge the wisdom of "upsetting the apple cart." If things are going well, they say, why argue with success? We all slip too easily into patterns of behavior that represent not so much what we want as our ability to adjust, to reconcile ourselves, to make do. Commendable as this may be, it's even more commendable to improve our status, and this is especially true for women. Too many of them live their married life so totally dependent—many even say, "I'll never make it without John"—that the transition to independence leaves them feeling like a basket case. It's more fitting to believe that a really good marriage will leave a widow more than mourning and despair. The growth she enjoys in a good relationship is, of course, temporarily set back by the grief over her loss. But if her marriage allowed her true growth and maturity, the widow will be left with the strength, the know-how, the self-sufficiency to carry on. She'll be equipped for a new voyage, even though its necessity was unwelcome. The smooth adjustment comes from having been responsible for herself, even when someone else was willing to do the job. It's a good habit to start right now.

Have You Become Too Dependent on Your Wife?

It's safe to say that most of us tend not to see the many ways, both large and small, in which our personal involvements leave us dependent on each other. In the marital relationship in particular, so much is shared in everyday life that it's easy to overlook how things really get done—it's enough that they do. We take a great deal for granted because what we don't do is done for us. Husband and wife develop a finely tuned division of labor, subtly directed more by tradition than choice, and remain blissfully unaware of how they'd manage without each other. In most cases, for example, a woman automatically cooks dinner, except when it's done on an outdoor grill. She shops for the food and her husband purchases the wine. This is changing, as most things are, but it's a slow process. Even though more and more married women hold jobs, men still largely preempt the role of moneymaker and manager. It is still the woman who has an uphill fight in divorce proceedings to come away with financial security. A widow, left with all her husband accumulated, is often overwhelmed by the intricacies of handling it.

In no way does this imply that the husband is free of dependency on his wife. The cost of living in terms of dollars and cents is easy to reckon. Money can be counted; it's handled by the simple process of addition and subtraction. But how does one establish the cost in time and effort of the countless services a wife performs for her husband? Seeing that the children are properly fed, clothed, and off to school on time; running the house; extending and accepting invitations; and marketing, laundering, purchasing gifts are only a few aspects of the woman's "job," not to mention her value as a lover, friend, and supporter. The list is very long indeed, and many men over the years, in their devotion to their own role in the relationship, become increasingly oblivious of the other side of the coin. There are some who could barely manage to find a teacup in their own home without their wife's help. Often their ineptness and dependency show up early, in the event of separation or divorce.

There is a large group of men whose business or professional accomplishments mask their domestic incompetence still further. The "importance" of their position endows them with a false sense of omniscience and omnipotence. They typically say, "Sure, what you say about dependence is obvious, but I'm different." Of course it's easy for them to be a good host—the preparation down to the last detail has been taken care of by the woman of the house. It's easy for them to take pride in their children—ninety-five percent of the time the children spend with their "parents" is with the mother.

Needless to say, these men miss a great deal by their lack of participation in the domestic side of life. They almost invariably go through episodes of despair over their marriage because of how little they seem to get out of it—an inevitable result of how little they put into it. They enjoy their own career growth but, without realizing it, expect their wife and their relationships to remain frozen in time. Most gloomy of all, the man's home never really becomes his castle if the place where he distinguishes himself most is his office. There should come a day when most of us will give up our office and not miss it. That transition will be rewarding only if our home has already become a significant part of our life and not something turned over to the custody of our spouse. Paying the bills isn't enough. Fulfillment demands more personal participation.

On the bright side, there are changes taking place in this area which offer promise. The increasing opportunities and freedom extended to women bring them closer to men. This closeness works both ways, in that men are also venturing into some traditionally feminine areas. The "waiting room" role for men during childbirth is often given up today for active participation in the act itself. Just as women now function on every level of business, professional, and political life, so men are encouraged to feed the baby, vacuum the carpets, go to the supermarket, cook—in short, to help and even become expert in areas that were formerly exclusively female territories.

There's no loss of status for men in this change. Some suffer from yesterday's prejudices and resist—only to lose out if they get their way. Love is best expressed not by poetic yearnings but by shared activities where, as in a musical composition, the whole benefits from the inner harmonics. People grow together not by declaring how much they mean to each other but by doing things with and for each other. The man who turned only half his life over to his wife cannot carry on without her. He hasn't developed the necessary skills. Worse than the dependency he developed is the fact that he never had all of his wife either. Having given only half of himself, he got only half of her in return. Arithmetic works differently in marriage. Two halves don't make a whole. Two wholes do, and each part is stronger and more independent because of shared experience.

The Marital Art of Scapegoating

Clinical psychologists often recognize that if we don't have symptoms, we probably have a scapegoat. A simpler way of saying this is that we tend to take our upsets out on others, rather than suffer alone. We needn't be aware, and generally aren't, but often we must admit that when we pick on someone, the amount of provocation is hardly proportionate to the anger we show. When a relatively trivial misdeed sets off a major outburst, there must be something else that has been building up. For example, a man may be justified in complaining when his wife gives him rye rather than the white toast he requested for breakfast, but if he has a major temper tantrum over it, you can be sure many other dissatisfactions and frustrations have found their way into the explosive charge. Even though he himself would dismiss them as irrelevant, other incidents—his wife's sexual rejection of him the previous night, her not wanting to go to the movie of his choice— have left him grumbling and unhappy with her. Or it might be disturbing things which she had nothing to do with that are at the bottom of his upset. The bridge partner he had last night, the attitude of the maître d' at the restaurant, traffic, persistent difficulty with the starter of his car—any of these could be gnawing at him, especially if for one reason or another he hadn't vented his feelings on the people who bothered him. (And there are some things you can't tell off, like your starter or traffic!)

To grin and bear it eventually affects one's appetite and digestion or causes headaches—in short, you develop symptoms. But this doesn't constitute an invitation to have tantrums at the expense of others. Venting anger that way is not nearly so therapeutic as it sounds. We may wind up with symptoms anyhow, and there is always the danger that sounding off irascibly will become habit-forming. Placing the blame elsewhere than with the cause of anger for the sake of venting our spleen almost always involves the selection of a "safer" target. The man in the example above didn't tell his bridge partner off or put the maître d' in his place. He spared himself what might have become socially embarrassing and, in the safety of his own home and marital relationship, let his hostile feelings out. He knows he may strain his relationship, but it's unlikely he'll be told, "I never want to play with you again," or "Don't ever come to this restaurant again"; so he has unconsciously taken the "safest" route—at his wife's expense.

Some of us do get more crotchety or irritable as we age (just as others mellow), and because it's relatively safe to do our scapegoating at home, that's where we do it. Husbands and wives are the number-one scapegoats of all times—the innocent victims of displaced or projected hostility. Oddly enough, although this is damaging to their relationship, it often becomes one of its most cohesive elements. The alternative of living alone can seem even more painful than that of being a scapegoat, precisely because there would be no one to complain to or about. But damage to the marital relationship is a high price to pay for alleviating the annoyances of daily life. There are alternatives to taking things out on each other. What we don't seem to know or come to terms with is that we live in an imperfect world and that it's naïve to let every obstacle throw us into fits. The existentialists have a better idea—accepting the absurdity of life and learning how to laugh at it.

Certainly not everything around us is equally important, and if we kept track, we'd readily see how often we allow ourselves to get as upset by small things as by more significant ones. This means we're unwittingly building up an explosive charge within us which will soon make us trigger-happy. Like the attorney who examines a contract to discover every loophole, we become sharpshooters determined to pick out everything large or small in life that deviates from what "should" be.

Emotionally, this is a costly way to live. A reshuffling of our values is strongly indicated. But this cannot be done by merely resolving to do so. It's not what's in our mind so much as our frame of mind that must be changed. Even an habitual scapegoater is sometimes in good spirits, and it's at those times that he's most apt to dismiss things that would otherwise bother him. This suggests that we should seize upon any and all small pleasures available to us. The more pleasure-oriented we become, and the more consistently we maintain our daily pleasure level, the more we'll dilute our stored-up hostility. Only then can we feel the relative insignificance of many things we overreacted to and recognize that we were making ourselves and our spouses unhappy by the importance we imputed to them. In short, the better we feel, the more pliable we'll become, and interestingly enough, we'll know we've succeeded by the greater number of smiling faces that greet us.

Separate Vacations
for Husbands and Wives?

Couples never consider going in separate directions on their honeymoon, do they? Why do many couples later feel the need to be apart on their vacations? What happened between then and now? Does wanting to be apart for a while mean a marriage is foundering? Is love waning or lost? Do you feel so secure about your relationship that separate interests can be indulged without risk to it? Would a vacation from each other really be desirable or therapeutic?

These are all valid questions, and it's not always easy to find the underlying truth. Strangely enough, people don't always know how good or bad their marriage is. (It's common knowledge that the reasons for much of our behavior frequently elude us.) We justify and rationalize more often than we truly explain our choices and decisions. But be that as it may, let's see where the issue leads. There may be more involved than first meets the eye in even a brief, innocent lark on one's own. Something integral to the anatomy of a marriage may lie beneath the surface of a desire for separate vacations.

I remember the case of a woman who told me how deeply she regretted "that first trip my husband made without me. It opened a Pandora's box of problems." It seems she yielded to his desire to join some friends on a five-day fishing trip into some remote sections of the Florida Everglades. Six months later, it was a white-water canoeing jaunt out West.

"Now," she explained with considerable exasperation, "he's gone every other month and we haven't been anywhere together in three years. Worse yet, we spend the time between his trips arguing about them. Life hasn't been the same ever since that first time."

Contrast this sad tale with that of a couple who found a new and better life together as a result of separate vacations. The man in this case went on a business trip to Florida, fell in love with a small city on the state's west coast, phoned his wife, and asked her to join him there. He was tired, needed a rest, and thought she might enjoy it also. She couldn't go because of some of her own commitments but suggested he take the rest of the week there anyway. The same thing happened the following year. The third year, he bought a condominium apartment, half on speculation and half because he really wanted to live there. His wife joined him on a subsequent trip, and they've been living together happily ever after in their new location.

These examples are at each end of a continuum of possible effects of separate vacations. In one case, the marriage was ruined; in the other, improved. Or so it seems. I add this last remark to bring attention to the fact that what happened may not really be a result of the separate vacations.

How much a man enjoys himself with or without his wife (and, of course, his wife with or without him) depends not only on his or her special interests but also on how much they mean to each other. It might also be said that while a moment of separation won't ruin a good marriage, it can hasten the decline of a bad one. The deep-down, vat-dyed color of a fabric survives even a drenching rain.

All too easily, we can mistake the mere triggering of an event for the major, underlying causes. The First World War was not simply the result of the assassination of a Serbian archduke—at least not from any sophisticated point of view. The powder keg, the explosive forces, must be there already for the trigger to release anything more significant than the pop of a toy gun. Long before the deed, the mere desire for a separate vacation needs examination. It's not unnatural even for people in fine working marriages to tire of each other from time to time. The problem is that many people do nothing about these recurrent moods and feelings. They figure they'll disappear as innocently as they came. And they do. But little by little, in an unobtrusive way, the sense of unfulfillment keeps returning. It festers and becomes more poignant. Soon we need someone to blame. Since every marriage has a built-in scapegoat, as we've seen, we end up thinking, "If not for her (or him) I could..." and we decide the time has come for separate vacations.

The point I want to make is that things are already too far along if we find ourselves grappling with the pro's and con's of separate vacations. There's a good chance we should really be acting on the much bigger question of what's missing in our life and/or marriage. We tend to allow things to worsen to the point where only some dramatic act of freedom or self-assertiveness, we feel, will do the trick. "All my life I've done what *you've* wanted. Now, for once, I'm going to please myself." Let's look at what's really behind that proclamation.

When a man complains that his wife doesn't share his leisure-time interests in golf, tennis, fishing, hunting, football, the stock market, his friends, his work, I hear not only the fact of his report but also the fact that he has failed to make these things attractive to her. Thus, the undesirable condition will forever remain unchanged. Similarly, when I hear a woman complain that her husband never goes antiquing with her, hates shopping, won't go to foreign or romantic films, despises French food, avoids concerts, lectures, and museums, and disagrees totally on resorts—I also hear what little influence she has had on him. Such people are already living largely separate lives whether they vacation together or not! How they spend their holidays seems far less important than how they are *not* spending the bulk of their life together. The real issue, then, is our basic failure to reach and influence each other more profoundly. This is where our thought and effort should go.

How do we go about increasing our influence on each other? Mostly by giving a little, then a little more, and then still more. This puts us in a better position to take a little, then a little more, and then still more. A woman who doesn't like to play golf can read about it, if it's dear to her husband, and then give a little by talking with him in an informed way about something he likes. She can give more by watching with interest at least part of a match on TV, and still more by riding in his cart with him one beautiful day. He can do the same with respect to any of her interests.

In this process of giving and taking, the couple increase the base of their companionship, feel the interest each is displaying in the other, and may even come to like what they formerly hated. Vacations soon become no more of a problem than any weekend or evening together. There are now opportunities for mutual enjoyment—not always to the same degree, but enough for both to want to be together.

By increasing their ability to share through the influence they now have on each other, husband and wife can take "separate" vacations together—and enjoy each other not only during them but, more important, during the larger part of their everyday life at home.

Better Sex after Sixty

The greater longevity we enjoy these days is happily accompanied by a degree of energy and vitality that was rare among the aged as recently as several generations ago. We now work longer and play longer, because our health has been more carefully safeguarded. Sexual research has proved that the most effective way to maintain our sexual ability, now that good health lasts longer, is by using it. In other words, if we want to enjoy a sex life as long as we live, all we've got to do is keep at it. We won't preserve it by using it sparingly, by treating it as though it were fragile. If we truly enjoy sex and have made it an habitual, robust part of our physical life, we can expect it to stay with us way beyond our sixties.

Today we have more reason than ever to enjoy sex after sixty because we're lucky enough to be alive at a moment in history when, at any age, better sex is available to all of us. Throughout the history of the Western world, particularly since the Renaissance, sex was suppressed so strongly that only the wealthy and powerful could please themselves at will. Ever since the now-famous U.S. Supreme Court decision written by Justice White suggested that "redeeming social value" be determined by local communities rather than by some supreme power, censorship has lost its power. Other forces in social life had been gently urging the liberalization of sexual attitudes, but the sober weight of a Supreme Court edict was exactly what was needed to take the giant step toward a significant difference in attitudes. A veritable explosion of sexual candor immediately followed in the media.

Most of us, however, were brought up with rules of morality and marked inhibitions which dictated the standards of good taste. Some people still look at sex as degrading, or dirty, an activity expressing our baser rather than our finer instincts. Even more people, liberated in their thought from such an attitude, still experience a lag in their feelings about the subject. They feel they've progressed a good deal, yet remain burdened by the inhibitions that dominated them for so long. It takes a long time to get rid of fears, prejudices, or judgments about anything, but until people allow themselves to give sex a good name, they will remain unable to enjoy it fully.

A change can be made any time in life, and now is the best time, regardless of age. The usual instinct is to point to one's partner: "I'm ready, but my wife (or husband)..." Often the biggest part of the problem is to convince ourselves and our partner that a great relationship isn't something we stumble on—we create it. We work on it with perseverance, gentleness, and inventiveness. The mistake we often make is to demand the very thing we ourselves are failing to give, and then to take refuge in self-pity.

Actually it's easier to improve the quality of sex when we're past sixty, because the decline in our purely physical needs is easily compensated for by the increase in our sense of emotional need for each other. In other words, what we may lack in physical robustness is made up for in tender feelings and love. Granted, there are people who live together feeding on the worst they bring out in each other, and there is little reason to expect improvement in any area with them. But most people fail to improve their sex life for reasons other than combativeness. First, their inhibitions dilute their efforts to contribute to a satisfying sex life. In allowing this to happen, they are failing to take advantage of the encouragement society, with its decline in censorship, offers. Second, people subscribe more than they realize to the myth that sex is essentially an activity of youth and doesn't belong to the aged. Third, we are so given to repetition that we bore ourselves and find someone else (our spouse) to blame it on. Fourth, we procrastinate: we put things off until we lose our motivation and don't know where to begin. The list can go on and on. The important thing is for us to keep moving, trying to bring about and then improve on what we want from sex.

Needless to say, the smaller the problem of sex after sixty is, the easier it is to solve. People who have always made sex an unquestioned part of their life have a small problem, if any at all. It's important to start improving now, since we can't do it yesterday. The fact is, sex is more acceptable today than it was a generation ago. We are less uptight about it. People of all ages enjoy more of it, not only through their own active participation, but in movies, TV, and magazines. In short, there's more encouragement for it than ever. All social behavior runs in styles. For a long, long time, it was the style to keep our language, our conversation, our visual arts devoid of direct sexual reference. The style has changed. Sex now enjoys a prominent position on the banquet table of social experience. Critics remain, and it's true anything can be misused. But if love is still highly valued among us, what possible objection can there be to its most eloquent physical expression in the intimacies of sex—at any age?

How to Make Your Marriage
Better after Sixty

It may seem presumptuous, if a marriage has lasted all these
years, to suggest ways to improve it. But age doesn't necessarily guarantee quality. And the fact is, we need and want
different things from marriage at different stages of life. The
great philosopher George Santayana once wrote that in marriage "passion settles down into possession, courtship into
partnership, and pleasure into habit." Romantics bristle at
cynicism and get their hackles up at this kind of statement.
But on more sober reflection, we must own up to the fact
that a stable, satisfying marriage of many years may long ago
have lost the mystery, sparkle, and passion of its early years.
However, we may no longer hunger for these qualities as we
once did. Certainly we remember them (a nostalgic grace
note prompts a backward glance), but essentially we're older
and different from what we were. Compassion, predictability,
character come to have value and supersede the early at-
tractiveness of things we now see as superficial. We hope
that these changes in taste and appreciation take place in both
husband and wife in tandem, that their relationship deepens
over the years, endowing them ideally with "a true partnership of feeling."

More commonly, however, the direction and rate of change
are different between marital partners. People can just as
easily grow farther apart as closer together. The reason for
this is that we are different no matter how much we share,

and different things happen to us in those segments of our life that separate us from each other. Additionally, even the best marriages are not totally without some areas of potential conflict, however well they work most of the time. All this adds up to the fact that marriage needs constant maintenance; no matter how old and well established, it cannot be taken for granted. My own experience in the field of marriage and family counseling suggests that marriages are never static. To keep a marriage alive, we must constantly improve it—even after thirty or forty years. The idea is not really an alien one; it's equally true of our bodies. The youth and vitality we enjoyed when we were young were virtually free. We hardly did anything to maintain them. Later on in life, we find we retain those qualities only by working at it: through diet, exercise, medical examinations, etc.

What are some of the effective ways to improve marriage after sixty? One of the characteristics of any sixty-year-old's life, married or not, is the huge amount of repetition in it. If a husband and wife were enjoined to reach out for some new experiences, new activities, tastes, and people, they would invariably come to enjoy added sparkle in their relationship. They would find a freshness that was missing when each day was no different from the previous one. Very often among couples of this age we find that one of them has worked things out well for himself or herself and the other is left out. In such cases, the busy one's program must be modified to include the other and/or help must be provided to fill out the other's life. The marriage is going to founder if only one of its participants is happy. Neither of these suggestions precludes a certain amount of independence from each other. It's perfectly healthy for husband or wife to visit family alone. Short periods of separation help establish a sense of self as well as an increased awareness of one's desire for the other.

Still another suggestion for improving marriage in our advanced years is to make certain we do not give up our active participation in the lives of others. Altogether too many people reduce their social contacts to a point where they spend virtually all their time alone together. If sharing is one of the outstanding characteristics of a good marriage, we must make sure we have things to share. Friends help the most in this area by adding their experiences to ours.

In many ways, it's a lot easier to improve marriage after sixty because of the greater freedom from the pressures of working life. But it's also easier, after all these years, to take a spouse for granted. The fact is, we need a good marriage even more now than before. We spend more time faced with it and no longer enjoy the daily satisfactions of other achievements. Marriage, we must be reminded, is not static; it'll get better or worse depending on what we do or fail to do about it. It's in our best interest to get cracking right away.

THE JOYS AND JABS
OF FAMILY LIFE

"Generation gap!" a friend exclaimed in a recent conversation. "You bet there's a generation gap. My grandchildren and I see eye to eye more readily than my own children and I do." It's reasonable to think of our children as mature when they're grown-up and have children of their own. And certainly nobody doubts our own maturity when we've reached the level of grandparents. Then why is the relationship between parents and their grown children so often less than mature? Is it because of our small tolerance for difference and disagreement? Probably. But other factors more specific to our roles also conspire to make things difficult for all concerned.

Among all human relationships, the one between parent and child is unique. First off, there is necessarily a large age difference between parent and child—an advantage at first and a source of enormous difficulty later on. Second, the closeness and warmth of the early years suffer small but constant erosion with the growth of the child, until finally he or she chooses to shift the focus of love elsewhere. What was once almost the whole of his life becomes a secondary part of it. Third, family life, unlike other social relationships, is dominated by moral judgment. At school, for example, children are graded and even failed if they fall short of producing what's expected. At work, people are fired or not promoted if they don't perform. Acquaintances may like or dislike each other and can freely express their opinions. But parents have the enormous moral power to make their children feel they are fundamentally good or bad, naughty or nice, right or wrong. This power can have two effects: it can leave children with a conscience heavily weighed down by guilt, and it can make parents feel like experts in control of minds other than their own. Grown children can't stand the absolute authority parents continue to assume, but may feel guilty about fighting against it. Finally, most of the parent-child drama takes place over the years in the home, a place where we let our hair down and are closer to our feelings than elsewhere. This can bring out the best in us—but often it brings out the worst! At home, extremes in our behavior become the rule rather than the exception.

All these conflicts do not prevent creation of strong familial ties. People don't have to agree and express affection to become dependent on one another. Even strong negative feelings have a binding effect—so long as they're given enough time. Family living generally nurtures both positive and negative feelings. This is what makes it so tricky. The grown child cherishes his maturity, his ability to make up his own mind, and he often sees his parents as meddling and overcritical, even though he knows they mean well. They're not his enemies, but they certainly can be annoying. Parents are often distressed by their grown children's inability to appreciate their good intentions and invaluable years of experience, even though they're aware of their children's general regard for them as people. The family begins to look like two groups of loyal citizens, Republicans and Democrats, commenting from opposite viewpoints on the same public issue.

Despite all this, being the parents of grown children can be more enjoyable and rewarding than parenthood during the earlier stages. Sure, we've been encouraged to look upon babies as cute, but we forget the bother and care their total dependency demands. First we spent endless periods of time cleaning them, then cleaning up after them, then just plain running after them. Even as they grew, there were problems, always problems—many threatening, others trivial but nerve-racking because of our overreaction and the depth of our commitment. These problems were wearing, and took more time away from the rest of our life than we would have chosen. Now, that our children are adults, they want only a part-time relationship with us. What a blessing! All we've got to do is accept this and enjoy the benefits of the principle that "less is more." The major obstacle is our resistance to change.

Many women gave up more of their lives to parenthood than they realized. And many men became more accustomed to their role of decision-maker than they realized. For a woman to become the parent of a grownup, she must fill her life to a point where she has little time or energy left for parenthood. And a man, like a successful executive, must learn to delegate authority and responsibility. Being a good wife and a good husband should always come before parenthood, even when children are little. And when they're grown, more effort than ever should be put into those roles.

Another fact we easily overlook is that our grown children tend to be the only young people we know. No matter how well we think we know them, it's preposterous to believe we can understand them if they are the only members of their generation in our life. Young people's standards and values, their language, their style, their very ideas about the quality of life may be—and often are—strikingly different from our own. This difference is not a matter of right or wrong; it's history and taste, pure and simple. It offers us one of the happiest opportunities of our life—to stay young ourselves by befriending young people. We'll get along with our own children better as a result. Why should anyone want to fight that? Why prefer being old and stodgy?

There are countless ways for us to defer to, rather than fight, the judgments of our grown children. We have every reason to accept their greater expertise in modern living even if we continue to believe life was better yesterday. They not only know far more than we do about the here and now, but they're also closer to the future. They're more a part of today's process of becoming; we have barnacles of the past clinging to us more tenaciously than we realize. Let us relax and encourage our children to take over. Urge your son to sit at the head of the table; it'll help you understand how he sees you. Let your daughter explain today's principles of child care to you; even though you may think your ideas are better, you must realize that they are better for you and not for her, given today's style of parenthood. Don't make the mistake of confusing best with appropriate. You may still be the expert on what is best, but if it isn't in step, it won't work.

Many parents get so used to being "misunderstood," "unappreciated," and "abused" by their increasingly independent children that the role of martyr becomes their métier. Even though it's a painful role, they don't want to give it up. They constantly justify their position by saying they're willing to suffer in the cause of right. What they fail to see is the self-defeating quality of being "right." They lose respect because they don't offer any. Love wanes and little more than a distant, distasteful sense of obligation remains in their children. As the relationship weakens and becomes more and more negative, it's harder to do anything to improve it.

But look how much easier and more effective it is to abdicate—well, not really abdicate, but accept—the role of volunteer rather than paid worker, elder statesman rather than responsible boss. You've got a life of your own to live. Just go along with your children for the ride. Ideally, your life should be full and busy enough not to allow time for more than the ride. Leave the planning, the driving, the servicing to your children. Lend a hand when they ask for it—if you're available. You no longer have to teach them; just enjoy them. Don't cluck over them; laugh with them. Become friends who used to be parents. And as much as you can, meet them on their terms. You'll find that your children, who beginning with their adolescence turned increasingly away from you, will once again grow close to you.

Don't Become the Child
of Your Children

We humans have the longest infancy and childhood in the whole animal kingdom, so it's not surprising that a residue of dependency usually lies latent within us once we come of age. By the time we approach our later years, we have a long history of looking after ourselves, and many of us also stubbornly insist on looking after our grown children, as the previous section pointed out. And yet there are dangers ahead of going too far in the opposite direction, of once again shrinking into a state of dependency.

Growing old is unavoidably accompanied by one loss after another. Even if we retire voluntarily we often feel we "lost" our job. Even if our health remains good, we feel a loss of strength, stamina, and agility. We lose some of our friends, and worse yet, loved ones such as parents or a spouse die. These experiences are deeply felt. They make devastating gaps in our emotional life. We can't divert our thoughts from our loss—we feel empty and deprived of the sparkle, the exhilaration of life. Soon we no longer respond the way we used to. Things seem less important. Our former alertness is gone and we take longer to answer questions. We rarely take the initiative; in fact, we're glad to have someone take over. In our slow surrender, we are allowing ourselves to become more and more dependent. What we fail to see is how high the price of that surrender is. Dependency keeps us in a state of depression, makes us prone to illness, and causes us to miss the opportunities that remain for the enjoyment of life.

This sad process of deterioriation is often aided and abetted by the good intentions of our children. For example, in their efforts to be solicitous of a widowed parent, they may treat him like an invalid. The amount of attention he gets makes the parent's new role appealing. The greater his obvious grief, the more righteous he feels and the more dependent he acts, thereby justifying the children's efforts. There are all the makings of martyrdom here. Inevitably the children want to get back to their own lives, but the parent is repeatedly hurt by anything short of excessive attention. The relationship begins to fall apart, adding still another loss to the bereaved's life. Even if his children sacrificed themselves totally to his wishes, his life would not be improved. All that sacrifice would accomplish is to bring out the worst in him. He would become cantankerous, demanding their attention instead of pleading for it. Neither is a happy state of affairs.

People maintain their vitality and productivity by virtue of their thirst for life and their will to live it. There have always been some people who do some of their best work well into their seventies and eighties, and nowadays there are even more of them. Turning yourself over to your children amounts to resigning yourself to a burial ground for the living. Not only are the children's lives unhappily obstructed, but your dependency on them is essentially an incarceration in grief. In short, nobody gains anything by the arrangement. Even if a parent becomes too feeble to remain the leader of his family, he or she can gracefully remain a consultant empowered to cast the deciding vote on matters pertaining to him or herself. The dignity in such a position is essential to self-image, a part of us that is often neglected and yet is every bit as important to our overall health and longevity as physical care. Self-image involves not only self-esteem but our store-house of motivation, values, judgment, and expectations. If we allow our self-image to sag, we lose yet another asset of our former life—namely, the built-in automatic starter we enjoyed for so many years. If we rely on other people to crank us up, we'll do less and less, until we finally fade away entirely.

What we do to remain independent and, more especially, how *much* we do will ultimately preserve the quality of our life. When we're alone, we enjoy ourselves most through involvement in projects, interests, hobbies, things to *do* which command our attention almost obsessively. The more driven we feel to discover or complete a project, to learn more about something, to work out plans, the less time we have for our pains and our complaints. Even feeling pressured is far better than having all the time in the world and nothing to do with it. But not all of one's time need or should be spent alone. If we allow enough people to populate our life, we don't run the risk of seeing our children as the lone oasis in a dreary, desolate desert. It's better to become so busy socially that sometimes we may not even have time for our children. Then when we do, our relationship will be all the more valuable. We will always be available to help out in any way, but we won't be relying on our children for attention, sympathy, or entertainment. The best relationship is always a two-way street, where the traffic can bear as much giving as receiving. The parent who allows himself to become the child of his own children is not giving, and so is risking a loss of respect and ruling out any chance of becoming a true friend. Friendship, which is based on *inter*dependence—not dependence—should be our goal.

Being a Live-in Parent

"It's not easy, not at all easy," a professional colleague of mine was saying, shaking his head from side to side to emphasize the difficulties. "And no one has all the answers," he added as we continued to talk to each other, sharing our experiences.

We were discussing the problems of live-in parents. The time may come when we find ourselves widowed and alone, ill and feeble, or just plain too old to look after our daily needs reliably. To a large degree the independence of our adulthood is eroded away by age, and it's not uncommon for us to feel neglected and abandoned. Feeling this way is itself proof positive of our loss of independence. Our children, on the other hand, can stand neither the guilt they suffer if they turn their backs on us nor the invasion into their privacy and life-style of having us live with them. What is there to do?

Let's start with the obvious: money helps. Compared with the emotional cost of recurring anguish and upset, money is the cheapest way to pay for anything—if you've got it. A live-in companion works much better than living with children—better for everyone. More frequently than not, a change of residence is also indicated. A smaller, more manageable place, one that is brighter and more cheerful, has accessibility to shopping, security, favorable climate, and offers the company of others in the 60+ stage of life, should be considered. We must do all we can on our own to preserve or, better yet, increase our sense of dignity and self-worth. After all, our fading self-image is already hurting our confidence and ability to act on our own behalf. This is the time to use what savings we have, because the help we pay for comes with the fewest emotional strings attached.

Sure, many say, but what if you don't have the money? If we have no choice but to live with our children, how can we make living together more viable? The answer boils down to weaving a pattern of opposites cleverly enough to make a single, harmonious whole. We must allow our children to enjoy an impenetrable space, yet maintain enough contact to feel wanted, at home, and part of their lives. It certainly sounds contradictory but, as in a fine piece of musical counterpoint, two melodies need not fight each other. They may in fact harmonize, even though they are able to exist independently of each other. In the case of the live-in-parent/ child relationship, it's especially important for us to remember to harmonize while guarding our own independence. We must reject the kind of help that might leave us with a craving for more.

Being invited to share a part of our children's lives presents the danger of accepting too much help. We must draw the line. If we permit ourselves to become the shadow of our children, we shadow our own lives. We should keep a respectful distance from their lives, which means we do *not* always have dinner together, we go out without them, and we encourage them to carry on as they did before we joined them. To this end, we develop our own outside activities. The well-adjusted adolescent spends more time with his friends than with his parents, and the healthiest elderly parents cherish a life of their own, no matter how close they may be to their children.

The largest part of the problem resides in us, rather than in our children. True, they can worsen the situation—often out of guilt, rather than compassion—by overdoing, over-giving. But if we constantly expect more from them, we erode our own self-sufficiency and become ever more demanding. It may sound irreverent and cold-blooded to suggest that goodness can be overdone, but the fact remains that our children do us harm by placing themselves in charge of our daily satisfactions. We cannot allow it. It's far wiser to teach them to remind us of opportunities, resources, tools, and allow us to take the initiative in using them. This is so even if we intend to share the activity with them. Let them know that we will make the necessary phone calls to friends and select the menu for the get-together they suggested. We can go downtown for the tickets. In short, we shouldn't hesitate to remind them of the responsibility we can assume. Only then can we expect to create the counterpoint of living to-gether and separately with mutual satisfaction. We have to nurture a relationship to make it rich enough to feed off; it keeps us alive because we keep it alive. We can maintain our identity while becoming part of something bigger than our-selves. All this is beneficial and healthy, and will improve the quality of our longevity.

Nursing Homes—Heaven or Hell?

Several generations ago, more people lived in larger houses and smaller communities. Often they stayed in the same place for several generations. It was easier for the aged and infirm to remain with their families. There was more space, safety, stability, and time for family life. Enormous changes have taken place since then. Most people now live in cities, with little space; there is far less safety, little community life, and families are dismembered and spread out over the country. The pace of life pushes us beyond the limits of comfort and keeps us in virtually a constant state of motion. People no longer have the time or the space, to mention the most minimal requirements, for undertaking the care of a feeble parent.

Is the nursing home, then, a viable alternative? Does it do its job for the people who take up residence there, or does it work only for the people who deposit their parent(s) there? Needless to say, there is no one solution for everybody. What one hopes to buy in a nursing home is a residence with watchdog care, company, and easily available medical services. Even at best a nursing home is not a home or a family. It's not everything the person who enters it wants, nor is it everything for the family who advocates it. But it might well be the best compromise available. The alternative of living alone can be emotionally destructive and physically dangerous. Living with one's children, as we've seen, can be even worse if it's felt as a burden. Nursing homes offer the opportunity for personal interaction, for the care of one's daily needs, for medical attention if needed—all without transporting yourself with great effort from place to place to get these things, and without placing an unbearable strain on your children's families.

The major obstacles people encounter in making the difficult decision about nursing homes stem from guilt and habit. Children who truly believe the nursing home would be the best choice are often prevented from saying so by a sense of guilt about "putting their parents away." If their parents react as though they *are* in fact trying to get rid of them, it becomes even harder to make the right decision with any sense of conviction or satisfaction. In the meantime, if the family are living together, things get worse between them and they become overwhelmed by the despairing thought that nothing will work. Habit, of course, always dictates that we stay as we are, no matter how acutely aware we may be of the inadequacies of the situation. Most cases probably remain unresolved due to our stubbornness.

More realistically, why not make an effort to find people with similar problems? Ask your doctor and friends if they know anyone you might contact to learn what experience they have had with nursing homes, retirement centers, living alone or with their children. Shared experience is one of the best bases for determining what one might try. Wherever possible, get a firsthand taste by sampling. Perhaps a week's trial might be worked out—at a nursing home, with one's children, or even with a friend. All the alternatives are so different from the way you lived most of your life that there's little reason to wonder at your initial hesitancy. But old solutions frequently become worn and ineffective. Even when we're least motivated to consider something new, it behooves us to keep one eye open to the possibility that we might like it.

In the final analysis, the best decision is made by the individual himself, not the people around him. It is we who have to live the daily life we choose. Whatever our choice, there will be irritants, rewards, trade-offs. We must learn that it is not the nursing home, our children's home, or our own that will determine the quality of our life. As Omar Khayyam put it, "*Myself* am Heav'n and Hell!"

Holidays—Family Fun or Fiasco?

We generally think of a holiday as a joyful, festive occasion; a time to eat, drink, and be merry. The picture we conjure up is one of people entertaining others in their homes, enjoying a relaxed openness, warmth, and interest in one another, all smiles and good feeling. At least that's how the pictures in the advertisements look. And it's a reality—for some. But when we get down to the nitty-gritty of holidays and think about them in a totally dispassionate, scientific manner, we must admit that although we're supposed to have a great time with the family, the truth is that many of us stopped having fun with them years ago.

We've seen that it's extraordinarily difficult to translate the parent-child relationship into a thoroughly adult one. We're too romantic and moralistic about family life realistically to alter its relationships with each phase of our growth. What is devotion at one point can become overprotectiveness at another. Our efforts to give our children the best can provide them with a happy childhood but an adolescence in which they find us overly critical and asphyxiating. We encourage their precociousness and independence when they're little and later resent being left out. By the time our children fly from the parental nest, they want some space and distance from it. It needn't be an act of hostility; they can be getting along fine with their parents, but other relationships interest them more now. Contact and sharing with Mom and Dad get to be less and less interesting. When a holiday comes up, they know they're expected to attend the festivities at home— and that wouldn't be so bad—but they might have made other arrangements they would enjoy more. This feeling is exacerbated by many things that people plan to do on family holidays.

A woman says typically, "I have to invite my sister's children. After all, I'm their aunt." The truth is, her own children have next to nothing in common with them and haven't seen them since last Thanksgiving or Christmas. Parents frequently enjoin their children not to invite friends on these occasions. "It's really going to be a family affair," they explain. But then their children's chances of having a good time are diminished.

The matter of the menu offers an opportunity to please grown children, but many women insist on turkey for Thanksgiving even though our Pilgrim forefathers themselves might have enjoyed lasagna more if they had known how to make it. We all too often allow tradition to dictate choices that have little to do with our tastes and preferences. Many traditional practices satisfied the needs of people in the society where they began. It was a simpler world, where the people who attended a large family dinner saw each other often anyway. They were friends as well as members of the same family. The choice of foods was more limited. And there was no outside entertainment piped into the home via television. Today, of course, the men are going to grumble if dinner is served as the fourth quarter of an exciting, deadlocked football game begins.

Holidays such as Thanksgiving and Independence Day, Christmas, Passover, and other religious occasions, as well as birthdays and anniversaries, can become opportunities for good times with the family—if we think them through and adapt them to today's world. The first requirement is to accept the fact that things are different today and that the family is not the same binding force it used to be. Start with that and you're off and running, because instead of a command performance, you're going to plan a party, the success of which is no longer taken for granted. *You* are going to make it good; tradition has little to do with it.

Instead of believing your children will enjoy the party because it's family or because they *should*, start by recognizing the obstacles and the competition. You know which people they like to be with; if you don't, find out. You know what they like to eat. You know what they don't like to talk about. All you've got to do is to recall the subject of every conversation with them that led to an argument. (No, it's not anything and everything you try to discuss with them.) The party doesn't even have to be at home. Take them (or let them take you) to the theater or to a restaurant of their choice. Tradition squeezes them into your yesterdays; instead, try to fit yourself into their todays. Have your own private Christmas, birthday celebration, or Thanksgiving on another day and show your children respect for their youth and their ways on the holiday itself. You might even find, to your pleasant surprise, that after several years they ask you, "When are we going to have one of our old-fashioned turkey dinners and invite all the other members of the family?" You know what? In the meantime, you might have learned to like the new format better.

The point in all this is that there's something more important in holidays than the holidays themselves. The meaningfulness of family ties is at stake. If we act unthinkingly out of pure tradition, it's the same as making the arbitrary declaration that strong family feelings of identity exist where they don't. Under such circumstances, the holidays become symbols and reminders of our unhappiness with family life. This is the very opposite of their purpose and our desires. Ideally, holidays offer us an opportunity to prove the durability of strong emotional ties. We do this best by showing our willingness and ability to share our children's lives, rather than dully expecting them to share ours.

The reward of this effort is that everybody has more fun, holidays get to be happier occasions, and even more important, we realize we're glad to have families with whom to celebrate.

How to Be a Grand Grandparent

There was a time not long ago when we didn't have to do anything to enjoy the respect and love of our grandchildren. Just being an elder—in fact, the eldest member of the family—was enough. The idea of an elder's place was built into a child's upbringing. It's a different world we live in now. Age no longer commands reverence, and authority is more often than not resented. It seems that the more affluent our nation becomes, the less we get for nothing. We've got to work for ideal grandparenthood today; it's no longer automatically endowed. On the brighter side, the work can also be fun, and what we achieve through it will be genuinely ours to enjoy.

Most people still like to believe that grandparents enjoy a free ride, that they're on the gravy train. They can play with their grandchildren and then turn them over to their parents when the going gets tough. They escape the burdens of illness, disciplinary problems, the countless chores inevitably associated with the daily care of children. The trouble with such generalizations is that they're too general. They may be true of the first few years of the relationship, during a child's infancy, but soon thereafter anything meaningful involves us in more than mere fun and games. It's demeaning to think of ourselves as mere fair-weather friends to those who give us a vicarious immortality. Even as children, grandsons or granddaughters appreciate us more if they feel they can talk about their problems with us. And we feel more loving and proud if they can.

The groundwork necessary for such a relationship grows out of our availability. This doesn't mean that, if we are physically close by, a splendid relationship is guaranteed. It's the closeness of our worlds, our interests, our attitudes that will make us close. Even when a grandchild reaches his majority, is old enough to vote, marry, have children, he's still—and always will be—years apart from us. He has different interests and attitudes. It's easy for us *not* to be close, especially when he is a child or teenager.

Now, who has the greater capacity to familiarize himself with the other's world? Does he? Or do we? The answer is obvious. It takes a long time to become an adult; it's much easier for us, with our adult skills, to learn what's important to the child. Yesterday's good guys and bad guys have to give way to today's heroes and villains. The same is true regarding sports idols, music, language, clothing styles, etc. The whole idea is to show so much know-how and enthusiasm for the child's world that he's perfectly comfortable in bringing his enthusiasms about it to us. If he has to reach up to get to us, he feels strained and inept. It's not an easy identification to make.

But it's not altogether easy for us, either. We're all more rooted in our past than we realize or is good for us. We tend to be contemptuous of much that is new and thus undermine our motivation to keep up with the world as it is. We keep making invidious comparisons with the "good old days." Whether they were indeed better or worse is not at all relevant. What our children and grandchildren hear us saying is that we are worlds apart, different from each other. That's certainly not the way to promote togetherness.

Something else we do, equally inimical to a close relationship, is to use our authority too much. We sit in judgment, correct, advise, suggest—put it anyway you like, but the fact is, we don't giggle often enough and accept our grandchildren as they do each other. We forget we're not bringing them up—they're not our children, and we're not their parents. Being grandparents sufficiently removes us from parental responsibilities so that we can be *friends*—really good friends.

Anyone interested in achieving such a goal with his grandchildren must understand two important characteristics of all young children: they have an extremely limited attention span, and they are addicted to a high level of activity. This means simply that they've got to be doing something all the time, something different. This is hard on us because we don't have to be constantly involved and certainly don't race around, jumping from one thing to another. Planning in advance is the best way to meet this dual challenge. Pitching pennies, a simple word game, a story, some riddles, jokes, a board game, exercise, doing things deliberately in slow motion, even tests of standing still, are some of the possibilities not to choose from but to use on a single visit. If you want to have fun and enjoy children, offer a smorgasbord of activities. They'll come back for more.

Accepting Kids as Kids

Respect for elders was always deeply embedded in our way of life. It was the same in all societies, not just our own. In the Orient, a culture much older than ours, people have always venerated age, and even the most primitive societies of Africa, South America, and Australia endow their elders with respectability. Just as we were taught to treat women and children with gentleness, so were we programmed to offer deference to the elderly. Their voices were associated with the wisdom of experience; their judgment was patient, their overall view had been broadened and mellowed by their years. The honor conferred upon them seemed deserved.

What happened? Do you often see a young man lift an elderly man's bag off a trolley at an airport or give an elderly lady his seat on a bus lurching in starts and stops through city traffic? Today young people shove and push their way past people their grandparents' age. Doors are allowed to slam shut on us; we get jostled, greeted with disrespectful salutations. These are common experiences. Worse yet, the elderly are regularly being attacked by muggers—because muggers are safer with them. What happened to our values that led to such a change in the behavior of the young?

Many forces and tendencies combined over the years to alter our established modes of behavior in a fashion no one planned. America, whose culture is becoming the major influence in the world, was almost always youth-oriented. Its stress on doing, moving, becoming, placed great value on the vigor of youth. Not only does athletic prowess (essentially a short-lived enterprise of youth) represent top achievement, but beauty itself has come to be defined as an exclusive possession of the young. This used to be balanced by the respect we had for age. But in the 1960s when the war in Vietnam came to the fore, youth rose in protest. They saw the war as an immoral abomination. Campuses all over the country led the attack against authority, right up to the White House. And authority, normally associated with age, suffered a severe blow. In addition, the immorality of Watergate destroyed the confidence millions had placed in our leader—a father figure and symbol of age and deserved authority.

All during this period, a third world of nations was emerging, placing into global prominence men of revolutionary character rather than elders who stood for the authority of law and order. These international and national movements may seem a far cry from the small, interpersonal matter of youthful rudeness. But the point is that the old order is being attacked, and in the heat of the struggle for assertiveness, the manners that marked yesterday's behavior seem less relevant.

More intimately related to our daily behavior are still other forces that have undermined respect for age and authority. The upheaval suffered by family life as a result of divorce (the statistics on which almost rival those on marriage) deprived parents of the special aura children ordinarily imputed to them. Parents became people—just like anyone else—no longer endowed with special wisdom and authority. It's become fashionable for children to make this discovery as soon as possible, even if their parents do not divorce, and they believe that they've reached maturity when they see their parents as mere relics of recent history. In fact, now teenagers feel more grown-up the more overtly they flout the authority of home, church, school, and even the law. They use their behavior as a mark of bravery and independence.

In light of these changes, large and small, lack of respect for elders begins to look like one of the more *minor* consequences. And it really is—but it's annoying nonetheless. It's also hurtful, because we feel less able as we grow older to cope with it. We expect to be treated respectfully because that's part of our tradition. We reject what is happening in the world as undesirable and place ourselves above it. But the irrepressible tide engulfs us whether we like it or not, and so it behooves us to learn how to handle the situation. The first requirement is to recognize the vastness of the changes around us. That is why, at the expense of sounding stuffy and academic above, I made reference to the historic forces involved. True, we all come upon young people who are still brought up in the old tradition: they're polite and respectful. But it's a mistake to be misled by these experiences and wishfully believe that the new rudeness is merely a passing phase. Unfortunately, a lack of concern for others is a style of behavior that's here to stay for quite a while.

Once we take the element of shock and surprise out of the offenses we suffer, it's easier to keep our cool. We can remain ladies and gentlemen even in trying situations. In a sense, it's the ultimate test of whether or not we really are what we like to think we are. Good breeding is vat-dyed; if the color is true, it won't run in the first sprinkle or, for that matter, even in a downpour. If we take pride in our dignity, we must maintain it even under fire. We're not going to change the world by allowing ourselves to be dragged down to the brutish level of behavior we abhor in others. The important thing is to keep our eyes on the target, this being our overall sense of satisfaction with the way we handle ourselves. Let's realize that "you can't win 'em all." Some things are feasible, and reality stamps others as not. We all suffer losses, but they can be tempered by how graciously we learn how to lose. And a smile not only helps us avoid becoming upset about losing; it is a splendid way of averting loss itself.

A Grandparent Is a Special Friend

Social relationships are generally created out of a recognition of some common ground for their existence. Having lived or worked in the same place, shared interests or causes, striven for similar goals, all bring people closer together. These discoveries of common interests are made, more often than not, by people in roughly the same age group. But children and their grandparents start their relationship with a whopping age difference. The gap can create many rough spots along the way to enhancing the relationship, and not all children and grandparents make it together. The differences between them are all the more difficult to resolve if the adults make no effort to meet the children more than halfway.

In the middle of a game of checkers, six-year-old Jimmy blurts out to his grandfather, "You stink!"

"Did I make the wrong move?"

"No, no," Jimmy says, pointing to his grandfather's mouth, "that stinks." Who else but a six-year-old would tell us about our breath that bluntly? Now we know why he turns his head when we try to kiss him and crawls out of our arms when we hug him. Even if we're offended, the fact remains that we probably do need a considerable amount of periodontal work. Those of us who are aware of the tactlessness of children may be stunned by their remarks, but not hurt or disappointed. We can accept their candor and do something to improve the relationship, rather than worsening it by bawling the child out for his "bad" manners.

There are many points of difference between children and their grandparents—at least as many as between children and their parents. Ideally, the roles for the several characters in this human drama should be specific and different. As grandparents, we are no longer charged with the responsibility of bringing children up. Even when they are temporarily left with us, we are not stand-ins, parent substitutes. It's a mistake to use such a time to start teaching them what we feel their parents have not. We corrupt our role and our relationship with them by becoming authoritative, demanding, and punitive. It's good for the child to have a relationship free of authority somewhere along the line while growing up in a world governed by adults. The experience is not unlike being served a filleted fish: you get a better chance to learn to like fish, uncluttered by its bones. Children obviously welcome this treatment—as they would a visit from Santa Claus. It's grandparents who all too frequently don't know how to stop being parents.

Role confusion spoils many a visit. A grandparent is typically horrified by a request for Coke at breakfast, but do you really believe a child's health or good habits would be ruined forever by a good-humored indulgence? And how do you think a grandchild feels about not being allowed to cross a street alone or to go into water over his head when his parents let him? Certainly he doesn't relish hearing again and again that he doesn't dress properly when he's got on the same jeans that he wears to school each day. Often, too, children are bored hearing grandparents tell the same stories again and again, the same "dumb" jokes, and repeating how things used to be. Not to mention how often they have to sit through interminable restaurant meals at boring places that don't even serve French fries, hamburgers, or anything else "decent."

There's plenty of time for our grandchildren to share and

enjoy our adult world when they grow up into it and become one of us. We are not amiss in giving them an occasional taste of it, but the better part of wisdom is for us to share *their* world. In that way, we become their only grown-up friends— a most distinguished and honorable position. The success we will enjoy as their friends need involve no loss of respectability. Grandchildren are generally aware of the age difference and know what we expect of them. They find it a relief that we don't exercise authority, and they will respond to us out of affection, rather than out of submission to threats and domination.

Many well-intentioned grandparents remain disturbed by the thought that becoming a friend may reinforce bad habits, spoil children, exacerbate their problems with their own parents. Maybe, but that's not likely to happen. If children do in fact have problems at home, it's all the more damaging to let them feel alone and friendless. Some link with the adult world becomes vital. Often a psychotherapist is the last resort, because there is no one else in the child's life to represent the grown-up point of view congenially. How lucky a child is to have grandparents he feels are friends, adults he can trust, who may disagree but (because they are never punitive) don't engender the horrible feeling that the whole adult world is against him. Because they bolster his self-image, grandparents create room for hope and for the effective use of his inner resources. Any good relationship has this supportive, nurturing quality, but frequently some of its other facets stand in the way. Grandparents are sufficiently removed from and, at the same time, close enough to their grandchildren to create something quite close indeed to the ideal of human interaction.

ILLNESS—
REAL OR
IMAGINARY

✥

Almost no one can resist the temptation to play up an illness: "When I'm sick, I'm really sick." I don't mean to promote the idea that we're all hypochondriacs—rather, I think that we are all varyingly hypochondriacal. The issue is generally clouded by oversimplification, by our feeling that we must be either sick or healthy. The fact is, we are usually sick *and* healthy at the same time. Something is wrong, but we carry on. Part of us is not functioning up to snuff, we may even be in pain, but overall our condition isn't bad. The problem is not so much a matter of whether or not we are sick but of how sick we are. Although physical medicine is capable of measuring "sickness" to some degree, it cannot do the whole job. It can tell us how far off normal our blood pressure, pulse rate, temperature, or blood count is. But it cannot accurately predict how long it will take a situation to normalize, certainly one of the measures of the severity of any sickness. Additionally, to exactly what extent we are suffering eludes physical science almost entirely. Nor can the psychologist, for all his compassion for human suffering, measure the amount any better. What he can do is help us see that illness does not exist by itself: it is always a particular individual who is ill. How sick a person is ultimately depends not only on what his sickness is but on what type of person he is.

Our attitudes toward health and illness, toward ourselves and life in general, play a large part in how we feel and act when we get sick. Some of us are apparently more prone to illness than others, feel pain more deeply, seem more fragile or tired, cannot take certain medicines, react more strongly to pressure, worry, or excess. Similarly, some people are more easily given to pessimism, despair, and depression than others. There are all kinds of sufferers: some with serious physical handicaps who remain vigorous and uncomplaining, others in good physical condition who never forget an illness they once had and live in morbid fear of getting sick again. This latter type tends to exaggerate the significance of any small distress. He or she blows up any discomfort immediately into a major threat to his or her health. A tiny pinprick suggests general blood poisoning, a sniffle becomes a harbinger of pneumonia, and a cough or two, tuberculosis.

Now we do from time to time suffer minor cuts, catch cold, or wake up with a sore throat. How we react depends not only on the condition itself but on how threatened we feel by it. It's very much like the different ways we can take no for an answer. Some of us feel rejected and disliked, while others see only a minor difference of opinion having no bearing on the quality of a relationship. Just as we commonly misunderstand people, we often misread our own physical signs. After all, multiple sclerosis, emphysema, and cancer are all realities. But there's a high drama in illness that can promote anyone from a pedestrian role in life—an extra, as it were, in a motion-picture extravaganza—to a star, cast as the innocent victim of forces beyond his control. There is in life no better excuse than illness and no quicker way to win the sympathy of others. That is what can make it so attractive. At the extreme, of course, illness can kill us, but more commonly it unleashes reactions that tempt us to exaggerate and perpetuate it.

A person need not be a dyed-in-the-wool hypochondriac

suffering from "imaginary" illnesses to react in this manner. There are weak spots in all of us. Illness is more frequent as we age, as are injury and pain. Changes in our status and in our self-image lead to self-pity and make us ripe for illness and its exaggeration. Someone once said old age isn't for children—or for sissies. No, it's a time to be tough. More than ever, we must work to maintain our health and vigor and a wholesome disrespect for illness. Imaginary illness or any imaginary part of an illness is just as debilitating as the physical condition itself.

If doctors had time to consider the person who is sick, and not just the sickness as some disembodied entity, they would be more successful in their treatments. By this reasoning, it's clear that we can help ourselves even more than our physicians can. A doctor determines what a disease is doing to us physically, but not at all what it may be doing to us psychologically. If our dissatisfaction with life is great, it clamors for expression. Our suffering cannot be borne silently forever— nor are there pills to get rid of it. And just as streams flow into rivers and rivers into the sea, so the things we fear and hate move within us, joining and seeking outlets in some socially acceptable form. Complaining loudly about a medical condition certainly allows some of this bitterness to escape. Not that it is done deliberately; none of us is conscious of everything that goes on inside our mind. But we can help ourselves even without total awareness and control. We'll do best by filling out our lives, improving their quality, and making a full life something we love. The busier we remain, the less time and inclination we have for illness—real or imaginary.

Living with Pain

Almost every year heralds new advances in medicine that extend our vitality significantly beyond the age at which our parents and grandparents enjoyed such good health. It's a source of continual amazement to find women in their eighties dancing until the wee hours, men still playing tennis in their seventies, and both continuing to enjoy significant sex lives. We no longer need search for a fountain of youth when an ocean of pleasures in age is open to us. There's little doubt that more and more people are in fact enjoying their senior years, but it's equally true that, as we get on in years, our bodily machinery tends to run down and cause us pain.

Probably the most common ailment is low back pain—the price we pay for enjoying our position in the evolutionary scale. Had we continued to move about on all fours, the way lower animals do, we might never have developed the pain that comes with our upright position. Additionally, we all suffer occasional bouts of illness, some of which leave traces of fatigue, discomfort, and even more specific physical reminders that we're no longer what we once were. Those reminders generally come in the form of pain. "Ouch" means "watch out—you're pushing yourself to your limit." We encountered fewer limitations earlier in life, but even then we had to heed signals of pain. The trouble is that even though we know such messages are important, they are not always specific enough to tell us exactly what's wrong or how wrong it is. Curiously enough, although pain is our major reason for seeing doctors, it is also the medical subject they know the least about.

Consider for a moment the fanciful idea that instead of hurting us, each "unit" of pain caused our skin to become a shade darker. Armed with a color chart, we could then measure more accurately the amount of pain a physical disturbance caused us. But even if we could measure pain by the unit, what would we have accomplished? Would we be measuring pain or our reaction to pain? Is there a difference? All this confusion makes treatment difficult. We all know that sound medical procedure dictates that we treat not the symptom—in this instance, the pain—but the condition which causes it. Yet look how often we settle for mere pain-killers, even though they can be addictive and, worse yet, can undermine what would be our normal adjustment to a condition that demands our best adaptive efforts.

Just because medical science—for all its progress—has not solved everything is no reason to settle for a life of pain and near-invalidism. First, stop thinking of yourself as the unlucky, innocent victim of an incurable condition. Even if that is true, such an attitude diverts your attention from anything you could do to alleviate your pain and invites you to feel sorry for yourself. We all hurriedly deny being crybabies, but it's true that the search for secondary gain is deeply rooted in human nature. What this means is that we soon discover that illness and disability are acceptable excuses for almost anything. People show us compassion, they feel sorry for us when we're sick. We can get more attention from them than when we are healthy, and we are expected to do less for them (and for ourselves). No one admits to enjoying pain, yet many build their life-style around it. They exploit their disabilities to evoke sympathy, and they succeed, even though they may be unaware of what they are doing. But the price they pay is steep. They end up limiting their life and suffering more pain than is necessary.

The most important strategy is to find out how much we can do despite our painful condition. Pills are often not nearly so good an answer as are the efforts we make to improve our life in general. Many people unthinkingly assume that once they are committed to daily medicines and a doctor's care, their whole life must be devoted to following an invalid's regimen. Nothing could be further from the truth! Let the doctor set the limits, but find out how much you can walk (or run), how often you can have sex, how much you can drink, what exotic ethnic foods you can eat, and what kinds of exercise and how much of them you can take. Often the sympathetic attitude of a doctor is misleading, and we erroneously infer that we mustn't do anything to strain ourselves. Soon this boils down to doing nothing at all. We don't walk, do errands, or carry things, and because of our sedentary state, we get weaker and weaker and become more and more the victim of our own pain.

The point is, rest alone does not get rid of pain. Sure, when we violently tear or break something in our body, rest is indicated. But total rehabilitation and general self-maintenance require both activity and rest. If the activities are not prescribed for you, allow your interests to be your guide. The two most important rules are be moderate and be self-observant. We all have the potential to get to know ourselves even better than our doctors do. See how much activity you can take. Don't wait until your exhaustion is extreme and you require a long recovery period; on the other hand, don't quit too soon. Always bear in mind that the activities that do you the most good involve some strain.

They should also involve people! Surrounding ourselves

with people can keep our mind off our pain even more effectively than engaging in solitary activity can. Crying is usually done alone; it is when we're with others that we're most apt to laugh. We're drawn outside ourselves into a larger, more objective world in which our pain takes up less room and seems less daunting.

A sensible program of involvement in activities and with people makes a most effective—almost magical—pain-killer. We get lost in what we're doing, and while we still feel pain, we learn to *live* with it, in the full sense of the word.

How to Be Sick

It certainly seems strange to consider the subject of how to be sick, given our deep, abiding interest in good health. But despite our desire to preserve health and vitality, the unfortunate fact is that sickness does hit any and all of us. Although we usually hasten to get well, as we have discussed, there are underground currents in our thought and behavior that may impede our progress. Assuming we have learned to avoid exaggerating an illness, we still need to learn how to be sick when we really are. The idea, of course, is not to learn how to get sick but to learn how to act and think when we are sick in order to get well quickly.

The beginning is easy. We simply put ourselves in the hands of others—doctors, nurses, any personnel necessary. At this point, they call the shots and we passively do their bidding. Generally, within a short period of time the responsibility for recovery shifts to us. We may still be in a hospital, or up and about at home. Weakness and pain, the side effects of medicines, dietary restrictions, and limitations on activity certainly tend to cloud our general outlook, but there's a good chance the worst is over. A diagnosis has been made and efforts launched at stemming and/or correcting our condition. Now is the time not to brood over what remains of the illness but to make sure we're doing everything we can to hasten the process of rehabilitation. The "good" patient is motivated to get well, while the "professional" patient always feels bad and flirts with the idea of remaining sick as long as the benefits of being a patient can be enjoyed.

The first step in restoring your health is to let yourself enjoy some of the things you gave up when illness struck. Laughter, for example. Tell family and friends to send joke books, and then learn to tell the jokes to others. Treat yourself to a concert or a new record album if music was part of your healthy life. Something imaginative and tasty to eat (if it's on your diet) can help brighten the day. Push yourself to do any exercise prescribed—activity is important. A crossword puzzle, a mystery novel, anything that steals your attention away from your illness speeds up the clock and brings you closer to the rhythm and pace of your healthy existence. Illness deprives us of much that we ordinarily enjoy, and unfortunately we often get carried away and learn to live with these deprivations. The best way to be sick is to continue to follow as closely as possible your normal, healthy, active life-style. With luck and good care, you'll soon find yourself back in the mainstream.

Dealing with Senility

We began this book by stressing that aging, like so many other phenomena, has both an up side and a down side. On the up side, many people today, as a result of improved medical care and the rise in our standard of living, live longer and maintain their vigor further into their life than people did in the past. Age frees them from burdens they bore through most of their years so that this final period is a gentler, more peaceful time, and the pleasures of a two-week vacation can extend year-round. On the down side of aging are poor health and loneliness, and they can exact a great toll.

Although the cures for some medical and psychological conditions are still unknown to us, we do at least attempt to understand the people afflicted by them and offer appropriate care. However, one illness in particular puzzles us: senility.

We understand the physical cause of senility—namely, hardening of the arteries of the brain, causing a dysfunction of the cerebral cells that handle our memory and thought processes. But who might be so affected and when we can't predict. Nor can we estimate the extent of the damage that may occur in a certain person. Worse yet, the symptoms come and go in no predictable pattern. An afflicted woman may not recognize her own son one day and yet recall details of his life he himself has long forgotten the next. It's as though the files of her memory bank have been tampered with; events that seemed to be misplaced or destroyed mysteriously reappear later in perfect order, playing havoc with her thinking. Facts basic to one's existence come and go in senility like mirages. Can you imagine how you might feel if on returning from the supermarket you suddenly wondered where you were? You had been sure you were on a street in another city, a city in which you did in fact live twenty years ago. Needless to say, you'd be confused, perhaps even panicky. Oddly enough, some senile patients in similar circumstances do not become alarmed, because what they've forgotten is so totally lost. Confusion then arises out of others' attempts to set them straight, and this can make a sufferer difficult to handle. Senile patients have as much conviction about what they understand as we do—often even more. Serious errors can easily be made if they take action based on mistaken beliefs: men have been known to alter their wills, leaving out their children or spouse entirely, without being aware of having done so. A custodian is appointed in many such cases to prevent a senile person from taking action based on irresponsible judgments.

There are also times when a person's senility can produce thoughts highly painful not only to his loved ones but to himself as well. When chunks of memory disappear and judgment becomes distorted, outlandish ideas begin to emerge. After an inconsequential scrap with his wife, a man who has forgotten he's on medication believes his wife is trying to poison him when she brings him his pills. She tries vainly to remind him that he's been taking these pills regularly for the last six months, but he obstinately refuses them in genuine and painful fear for his life. Two days later, he may accuse his wife of neglecting him because she hasn't once reminded him to take his medicine. There is simply no consistency. All we can do is be patient, roll with the punches. In some cases, like the one just described, the lapse in memory is accompanied by fearful misreadings of the behavior of others. In other cases, senility can be benign and the sufferer will allow, even encourage, others to help him with his recollections and present orientation. It is best to accomplish this the same way we would help someone across a busy thoroughfare: lead him across, but don't lift him up and carry him.

General talk of senility often raises questions among 60 + ers about the keenness of their own mind. Many elderly people own up to a decline in the capacity of their memory and some even wonder if this is going to get worse. They may even joke about having become a bit senile. But they actually *do* little to improve their memory. They approach loss of memory with much the same attitude as they approached other changes that come with age. A man complains, "I get tired after just strolling down my street to the brook. When I was younger, I used to walk for miles without fatigue." Examine his life and you discover he spends more and more of it on the seat of his pants. It isn't that he gave up walking because he tires too easily, as he claims. He got tired because he gave up walking! The same thing happens with our mental skills. If we allow them to lie unused, we can expect them to desert us. Memory needs maintenance.

A memory is created when we see or hear something and give it a place in our mind. The event may be small, passing, and unimportant, or it may be something large, colorful, and exciting. The amount of storage space we give it is dictated by its relative weight. Each time we refer back to the memory, the path to it widens and it becomes more accessible. It makes sense, then, that small events of the recent past are easily lost in memory. They don't occupy large spaces in our minds and the paths to them are not well trodden.

Many of the elderly say, "Those small events don't bother me. It's my forgetting significant events of yesterday and the day before that worries me." Remember that the same principles of memory hold here. Events are not small or large, colorful or dull in themselves; it's what importance we attribute to them that counts. If we've allowed our days to become empty, unplanned, and meaningless, and allowed ourselves to become inactive, uninterested, and inattentive, *nothing is going to register*. It's not our memory that is deteriorating—it's our lives in general. Little by little over the years, we have abandoned more and more of our physical and mental maintenance programs. We exercise less, listen less, become less and less interested in causes and goals—in short, we sow less, and "as we sow, so shall we reap." We cannot allow our memory to lie fallow and then express despair over how infertile it seems.

Granted, it's not easy to reactivate something we've long neglected, and it's up to each of us to decide how badly we want to. Some people believe we prepare ourselves better for the end of life by letting it run out slowly. But most of us do not lose our appetite for the banquet of life—we savor the dessert with the same relish we had for the appetizer.

How to Beat the Blahs

We all know what it's like to wake up one morning after a fitful night's sleep feeling simply blah. We don't feel like getting up out of bed and yet we're not comfortable staying in it. We're mildly irritated, yet not strongly or specifically enough to fight it or complain about it. Nothing seems right, yet nothing's really wrong. We feel there is *nothing* to do. Why get up at all? Suddenly all our paths of action have vanished. Which way do we go? Why bother choosing?

Although this kind of depression is not totally unfamiliar to anybody, some of us are more prone to its bitter taste than others. During certain periods of our life we are all especially susceptible to it. In old age, we tend to romanticize the past— everything was better and brighter, and more important, we were busier. Life seemed to spread out limitlessly before us, sweetening our days with hope. Now we feel it's a struggle to face each endless day. What we need are some defenses against the blahs.

Three of the most effective blah beaters are: activity, maintaining a sense of anticipation, and finding and satisfying our personal pleasure level. How can we identify and strengthen these conditions in ourselves? Take the first one—activity. A friend complained, "I'm not so young as I once was. I had to give up tennis after my hip operation. I didn't want to quit working, but I had reached the age for compulsory retirement. And the fact is, I'm tired most of the time. Tell me, what can I do under these circumstances?"

"Okay, I will," I said. "Your statement implies that playing tennis is the only way you can be active and that being at work is the only way you can be busy. Instead of tennis, how about shuffleboard, gardening, cabinetry, sculpting, automobile mechanics, bird-watching, or photography? Instead of requiring a job to keep you occupied and busy, turn to any and all of these activities and soon you'll complain about not having *enough* time. Before you reach that happy state, you can take advantage of having extra time." Another suggestion: we all get exasperated by the difficulty of finding a place to park when we do errands, or go to restaurants or the movies. Why not leave earlier, park a distance away from the crowds, and enjoy a leisurely stroll in an area different from where you usually walk? The things we do for ourselves need not be done in the same pressured way we did things at work. We used to complain about that, remember? Now the burden of deadlines has been removed, and we're free to do as much or as little as we want. We can remain active but decelerate, pace ourselves, slow down enough to allow our feelings more expression than they once had.

Bob W., for example, got a real-estate license and decided to try his hand at part-time salesmanship. It happens that the area he chose to live in when he retired was booming. If he had allowed himself to, he could easily have worked fifteen hours a day. "I almost did," he commented while fishing one afternoon. "I got carried away by the amount of business available and, I suppose, by my own long-standing work habits. Fortunately, I saw what was happening and I put a lid on it. Now I take my time; I enjoy my customers as people, and I sell only the houses I believe have real value. This is really the way to work—and live." There's always more to see and more to enjoy when we take our time.

The second defense against the blahs lies in developing a

realistic sense of anticipation. Once a person realizes that he needn't live forever to live well, he can easily look forward to tomorrow. The trick is to start thinking of only tomorrow— not of what things are going to be like ten years from now. There's more we can do about short-term goals, and thus they have greater impact and influence on our lives. Phone a friend—right now, before you finish reading this sentence— to make a date for lunch, a stroll, or a movie tomorrow. Once you've done it, tomorrow no longer looms before you in a vacuum. You'll find yourself in some small way actually looking forward to it. You've begun a process. Soon you'll make dates for next week, next month; even plan a trip for next season or next year. Your tomorrows will take on meaning. We tend to forget what a forward thrust our earlier lives had. We were always looking toward graduating, getting a promotion, getting married, having children, watching their next phase of growth, their graduation, etc. There's no reason for us to feel that we've come to the end of the road now.

Finally, we can avoid the blahs by watching our diet—I mean our emotional diet. We cannot afford to forget certain necessary nutrients. We mustn't allow a day to pass without indulging in a chuckle, even if we have to go out of our way to find one. Laughter is not a luxury—it's available to all. A delicious taste, a pretty sight, a pleasant sound, a novel idea can all help make us glad to be alive. They are the personal indulgences we must seek. We cannot depend on them to find us; we must look for them, steer in their direction, because as we make our enjoyment of life richer and more habitual, we leave less and less room for the blahs!

What, Me Worry?

Even the most confident and optimistic person worries once in a while. He can't help it. The reason's simple: none of us, no matter how wise or experienced, can see far enough ahead to be totally comfortable with the future. Even if we feel in control, that control is never total. "The best laid schemes," as the poet Robert Burns warned us, often go awry and leave us with "grief and pain for promised joy." So it's quite natural for us to worry when things important to us are at stake. A real worrier, however, feels this way too much of the time, maybe even most of the time. He's become a professional at ferreting out the elements of uncertainty in every situation with such obsession that he's constantly in a fearful state.

Life is tough for a worrier. He sees the shadows while others enjoy the sunshine. He feels the sting of disappointment even before things go wrong. There's no part of his life that is not constantly threatened by an avalanche of calamities. His own insecurity is so great that he doesn't believe there *is* any security. He sees people who don't share his alarm as foolish. Such an orientation toward life limits the amount of joy he might feed on, and his fears frequently eat into his own body. It's not uncommon for the worrier to suffer from any of the well-known psychosomatic disorders such as headaches, frequent colds, heartburn, indigestion, ulcers, etc.

The way someone gets to be a worrier is simple. For one thing, the trait easily rubs off from parent to child—not through heredity, but rather through shared experience. Hang around a worrier long enough and you too will become alarmed. There are also many other, far more subtle psychological circumstances that conspire to leave a person fearful rather than accepting of life's challenges. Early feelings of rejection stemming from feeding problems, the birth of a sibling, the absorption of parents in their own work and lives — to mention a few of the potentially damaging experiences of early life — can predispose a child toward insecurity and fearfulness. Unfortunately, these feelings are easily reinforced by subsequent experience.

Understanding the origins of worrying is at best an academic exercise. What's more important is to learn what to do about it. We've already discussed what worrying does *to* us. Let's pause for a moment to consider what it does *for* us. This kind of understanding will be more useful in modifying our behavior. Worriers enjoy being able to impress us with their knowledge of the intricacies of a problem. Their fear has prompted them to research them much more thoroughly than we may be inclined to, and they use their knowledge to twist their insecurity into something positive. This makes them feel superior, and they derive satisfaction from using the smug phrase "I told you so." The desire to impress us is not abnormal, but it is an unhealthy form of compensation for the crippling effects of worry. Worriers need to realize that there are easier and less personally costly ways to impress a friend.

No amount of talk or counseling is going to change a worrier, but laughter might! If you are a worrier, you probably don't find much to laugh about, but you should let yourself share what others find funny. We relate to others in a far more gratifying way by participating in the joys of living than by moaning about the inequities and shortcomings of our world. If you don't experience much of the joy of living, find people who do and plant yourself among them. You won't immediately get rid of all your worries, but you'll find lots more time for laughter. And you'll be off to a healthy beginning of the end of your life as a worrier.

Are You a Normal Neurotic?

As you might expect, people have reacted to the question above in a variety of ways. Some find it amusing, others are puzzled by its apparent self-contradiction, but most say, "Normal neurotic? Yeah, that's me; that's just what I am." They find, surprisingly enough, that the term fits. It's a diagnosis of themselves they can live with; namely, that they're not totally normal (because they're not satisfied with their behavior all the time) but that they're not hopelessly neurotic either (because they are responsible, functioning individuals who often enjoy life). In short, they're both normal *and* neurotic—normal neurotics.

Consider what happens if we're forced to think of ourselves as either normal or neurotic exclusively. If we are convinced we're completely normal, we'll have little motivation to correct our shortcomings. We'll take refuge in our good intentions (the road to hell is paved with them) and in being "right" (small comfort if no one else agrees with us). If, on the other hand, we accept being neurotic, we are often tempted to disclaim any responsibility, characterizing ourselves as the unfortunate victims of what others (usually our parents) have done to make us this way. Thus, the diagnosis of being just one or the other—normal or neurotic—locks us into a state promising little or no growth and improvement. By avoiding the either/or choice and seeing ourselves as *both* normal and neurotic, we open ourselves to the opportunity for self-help.

Now that we have "diagnosed" ourselves and recognized our ability to act, we must do so. The schoolchild who says, "I never could do math" and gives up never learns how. It's only through action that we get something up on the scoreboard. Take, for example, a man who has developed a fear of flying and as a result simply won't get into an airplane. He's not going to overcome his neurosis simply by reading about phobias or talking to friends, doctors, or clergymen. He will do it when he faces up to the fact that he isn't afraid of the dark, large dogs, driving over bridges, traveling through tunnels—in short, he's not a generally phobic person. The way he's got to learn not to be afraid to fly is by getting into an airplane. Of course he's going to hate it at first, but the idea is no different from the simple fact that the only way to learn how to swim is to get into the water. By refusing to allow our fears to immobilize us, by simply doing what we have to, we will overcome fears and even learn to enjoy many of the things we used to avoid.

The point is that having a symptom doesn't necessarily mean we're sick. Real mental illness is an immobilizing, complex state that requires treatment. Most of us merely have isolated symptoms—we're normal neurotics. In our condition, we can (and must) treat ourselves. But not by becoming psychologists! We've become overly sophisticated lately in our accumulation of psychological knowledge. But we've learned what the doctor has to know, not the patient. We can't really help ourselves by understanding about oedipal attachments, unconscious strivings, and sibling rivalry, any more than a medical doctor can improve his health by understanding the biochemical basis of disease and deterioration. It's the *use* of such knowledge, how we act on it, that counts! The rule is simple: if we don't get what we want out of a situation, we must try something else! Just sitting still and feeling righteous, unappreciated, unlucky, or scared isn't good enough. And merely repeating our unsuccessful performance simply isn't in our best interests.

Do something different! Keep doing, keep trying, keep your eye on the target—the target being the satisfaction of getting what you want from life. Generally this involves relating better to people, whether you like them at first or not. As you get to know them better, you'll come to like them better. And as you raise your daily level of satisfaction, you'll become increasingly more normal than neurotic. There'll be less clash and conflict. We can keep the emotional cost of living from constant inflation. Life will be less of a struggle and more of a gift.

How to Work at Being Healthy

Most of us enjoy good health while we're young and so grow up taking this precious possession for granted. Maintaining our vigor and recovering from minor injuries always seemed to require no effort. Vigor was a given, an asset that regenerated itself. Sadly, as we all know, over the long term our bodies wear down, change with age, and can no longer be expected to perform as they once did. This decline is unhappily accompanied by lingering fatigue and pain, and calls for a modification of self-image we are all reluctant to make.

None of this implies the loss of basic good health. No matter how old we are, we can remain healthy. True, our physical goals must be trimmed, but we do hold on to most of our skills. The major difference is that what we got for nothing in our youth we have to pay for now that we're older. At eighteen, you could tumble out of bed and play tennis all day. At sixty-eight, you've got to do thirty to sixty minutes of orthopedic bending and stretching to develop the flexibility to play for two—not eight—hours. We do pay, but because of the skills we developed over a long life, we may actually perform better (if for a shorter time) than the young man fifty years our junior. If we stop to think of it, the cost is not out of line. An eighteen- or twenty-year-old pro, in his desire for a super performance, pays a price in his strenuous exercise, limbering up, and practice. We who are not so interested in setting records have no need to strain ourselves. It's all a matter of degree.

Once you recognize and accept the value of being healthy, there are things you must do to achieve that goal. You should visit a competent general medical practitioner several times a year. Diagnostic tests can reveal internal processes that you might not be aware of until they reach an advanced state. Additionally, your doctor can act as a medical traffic director and send you to specialists to make still other observations necessary for good preventive care. It's a bother and an expense, but if you consider how many years you managed without close medical attention and amortize the cost over your whole life, it doesn't amount to all that much.

Any physical maintenance program ideally involves some fairly vigorous physical activity—enough to sweat over—on a regular basis. Our bodies fall apart from disuse more than from any other cause. Early in this chapter we met a man who had walked miles in his youth and now was complaining that he could hardly walk several blocks without tiring. We examined his life and found that he spent 98 percent of his waking hours sitting. If we want to feel the zest we once derived from activity, we must continue to sweat over that activity—modified, of course, to suit our age. Needless to say, exercise can be social and enjoyable at the same time that it's healthy. Keeping our weight at a respectable level makes activity (as well as the doctor's job of keeping us healthy) a lot easier.

Good health is not all physical. It's intimately tied up with how we feel about ourselves and the world. Our psychological well-being is all part of it and, under normal circumstances, does not require the help of a doctor. It does require the help of other people. Nothing guarantees our emotional health like a social life. How often does our phone ring? How often do we have lunch or dinner with friends? How often do our days include laughter? Friends and laughter go together; we don't laugh alone, and laughter is the most pleasant human sound to reach our ears. An additional advantage to being with people is that it helps us be more adventurous. We tend to hazard much less when we're alone and, as a result, fall into a pattern of repetition and boredom. New experiences add sparkle to life, make us feel young again, and leave us with a sense of greater fulfillment. We all suffer more inertia than is good for us. It's a big world out there, with many attractions. We've got to move, even push ourselves to reach for them. It's all part of the price we pay to stay as much alive as when we were younger.

A reliable overall indication of good health is *not*, oddly enough, a clean bill of health from your doctor. Even given that assurance, you can feel tired and achy most of the time. A better indication of health is that you don't have enough time for all you want to do. I refer, of course, not to your work life, but to your leisure time, whether you're retired or not. A famous psychiatrist used to suggest as a formula for the good life: "Seize upon a cause and follow it." The more involved we are with causes, interests, ideas, activities, and people, the richer—and healthier—we are. This is when we enjoy life most and are least bogged down with anguished self-awareness. The state of mind goes by many names: Nirvana, good adjustment, mental health. The secret of finding it is in attaching ourselves to the life around us, not to ourselves.

LIFE MUST GO ON
. . . AND CAN

Knowing that we may all get sick and will eventually die doesn't seem to help us much in adjusting to these contingencies. Nobody prepares emotionally. At best, our anticipation of the debilities that can occur with age prompts financial planning in the forms of insurance and savings, but little else. How a man and woman will live together when one of them is seriously ill or how one's life will go on after the death of a partner are hard issues to face ahead of time. But they're even harder to face once they've happened.

What exactly are the emotional difficulties involved in coping with an illness that renders husband or wife unable to function? What happens to the other when one of them becomes bedridden with a long illness? Of course, everyone's heart goes out to the patient. But what about the spouse?

At first, his or her concern is almost totally for the person who is sick. For example, a man makes every effort to marshal the best expertise and care. He seeks out all the information available and spends a lot of time with his sick wife. After a while, his relative helplessness overwhelms and depresses him. Soon he becomes angry—first with the doctors, later with himself, and eventually even with his wife! The monotony of each day, particularly if it brings no new hope, gnaws at his patience and robs him of the anticipation of anything joyful. He feels abandoned by his luck and his wife both. In a way, he feels he is already dead, while she lingers on.

Along with his frustration, depression, and hostility, the husband finds himself grappling with such questions as "What more can I do?" "Did I do the right thing in my choice of doctors and hospitals?" "Should I be spending more time with her?" "Should I accept the occasional invitation to dinner from friends?" Feelings of guilt and discomfort are apparent in these questions. Thoughts of his wife's death haunt him, seeming to accuse him of wishing for it. During this period of rumination and despair, he does nothing to maintain the quality of his normal life.

If it's the husband who is ill, the woman generally fares somewhat better. In most families, she has been closer to the business of creating creature comforts than he has—and she's been at it for a long time. The household still runs smoothly, because she's in charge, and she can more readily maintain a semblance of her past life. If the man is still employed and can remain so when a long illness befalls his wife, he too will survive it much better, because he's not thinking about her health problem full-time. In other words, we all adjust best to dire illness in the family by holding on to as much of our former healthy life as possible.

Some people are quick to criticize this attitude in a super-righteous manner. "Do you mean such a man should go out dancing while his wife is bedridden? Are you suggesting he turn her over to paid help and go his merry way?" It's easy to be "holier than thou" when you're looking in from the outside, but there's really little compassion in such criticism. The biggest mistake is to be drawn to extremes. For the healthy partner to become a martyr to his spouse's illness is as unproductive as neglecting him or her totally. The latter is morally reprehensible; the former is self-defeating.

There is a middle ground that makes good sense. Enough sacrifice should be made to assure proper care of the patient, and enough time should be given over to yourself to keep your spirits alive. After all, the healthy person must stay healthy! This requires a certain amount of activity. Just as we have to eat and sleep, we also have to socialize and move. Just sitting constantly at someone's bedside amounts almost to an adoption of the illness, not a cure for it.

The same philosophy applies to the death of a spouse. Many a man or woman continues to live totally in the memory and effects of the deceased partner. Here, too, reason has been easily crowded out by going to extremes. For a while, assuming the illness has not been very long, we expect people to succumb to their mourning. But:

> The Moving Finger writes; and having writ,
> Moves on: nor all thy Piety nor Wit
>   Shall lure it back to cancel half a line,
> Nor all thy Tears wash out a Word of it.
>   —*The Rubáiyat of Omar Khayyám*

Mourning expresses grief, but it does nothing to remove it. Life must go on—and can.

Just as tradition is best served by continuing to do the best of what was done yesterday, so is the memory of a person best served by living as one did before his or her death. Keeping yourself in mournful hiding is a violation of the memory of your spouse. We need others, especially in grief, in order to recapture our life's earlier quality. The sooner we reach out for them, the more fully we can once again count ourselves among the living.

Mourning

We have no difficulty understanding why the loss of someone with whom our life is interwoven is so hard to take. Love and habit are two of the most cohesive forces we know. It can be overwhelmingly difficult to rearrange our emotional life to absorb the deprivation caused by someone's death. Particularly if it's a child, a wife, a husband, or a parent, the difficulties can be extraordinarily deeply felt.

The picture is often complicated by feelings other than love—feelings we don't like to recognize in ourselves. Guilt has a way of lurking in the shadows of our being, causing enough discomfort to drive us in strange directions. A man may feel ashamed deep down inside for having neglected many of the wishes of his wife or mother when she was alive. Out of this sense of guilt, he may overreact to her death, feeling as though he was somehow responsible for it. His outward expression of grief suggests to the world the enormity of his love, whereas he is really suffering so much to satisfy his need for punishment. And punish himself he does—by renouncing the world and its values, by turning inward so that his relations with others decline, and by expanding his grief into a devotional state for an overlong period of time. All this adds up to depression—a deep, dark emotional abyss from which one does not easily emerge.

Needless to say, this type of mourning has no functional value. Nothing gets done except to keep pain and suffering alive. If there is any time in life when we are in danger of being too literal-minded, it's when we face death—our own or others'. We should use this time to memorialize the spirit of a person. If he or she stood for the good life, for equality, for love, for achievement, for understanding—for any one or several of these—that spirit is what can remain with us. The person may have "shuffled off this mortal coil," his body, but we can keep him alive in spirit by acting as he would want us to. The expression of grief doesn't celebrate his memory nearly so well as continuing to live happily does.

Although mourning generally requires a period of privacy, hopefully brief, it's people and activity that will help us move on to the next phase of life. By directing our attention outward, they help prevent the past from invading our thoughts. If adjustments have to be made in our behavior, we're better off thinking and talking about our tomorrows than our yesterdays. We must get back in the driver's seat, so to speak, instead of floundering in the trauma of loss. Of course, it's hard to be sensible when your heart is heavy, and it's equally hard to resist feeling sorry for yourself. But if you discourage the efforts of friends to help pick up the pieces and get on with your life, you will do yourself injury. Constant mourning is not an acceptable life-style. And even if you believe life will never, never be as good for you again as it was before your loss, it behooves you to make what you can of it, to come as close as possible to what you once had.

Some widows and widowers maintain their styles of life by a fortunate remarriage. Certainly there are adjustments to be made, but remarriage offers the greatest opportunity to preserve one's life-style. Without a new partner, holidays, weekends, even ordinary evenings can be difficult to face alone.

Some other radical change may be indicated to take one's mind off grief. Often for women it takes the form of adopting a career. A mere job (rather than a career) may turn out to be too routine and dull, leaving a woman feeling sorrier for herself than before. A career involves more of an investment of self, stirring up motivation and an interest in tomorrow. It may require an investment of money, time, and certainly effort, but it's not too late, no matter how strongly some protest. Men often find themselves in the same boat. Although a retiree may be able to return to work in his field, a new and less demanding area may actually serve to fill his need for a central focus in life.

The death of someone we lived with and loved need not terminate our love or our life. We can continue to love that person even if he or she is "replaced," and we can continue to live with his or her memory. We must realize that the death did not take place in order to "punish" us in some way. We make it seem so if we incarcerate ourselves in mourning for the remainder of our life. Life has meaning only when it is lived, despite the obstacles. We owe ourselves a certain amount of satisfaction, and we owe the people around us a certain amount of responsiveness. These must remain the pillars of human existence, even in mourning.

The Art of Living Alone

Living alone is rarely an act of choice. Convention and preference almost always throw us in with other people, and that's how we live our lives. Not that we're always happy about it— we also treasure our privacy and at times like to be by ourselves. An empty cathedral, an unspoiled beach, a fresh snowfall in the woods, all offer a silence, a respite from the incessant noise of civilization. We may feel closer to our feelings and thoughts in such solitary settings. But loneliness is not our natural state. We're drawn to what we're most used to: people. Even men and women who divorce usually remarry, because although they may have become disillusioned with their particular partners, they are still attracted to the idea of sharing life with someone. Of all the people who live alone, it's the person whose marital partner has been stolen from him by death who feels his loneliness most poignantly. He feels none of the comfort springing from the voluntary dissolution of a bad marriage. Nor does he enjoy the privacy and freedom of being by himself, because his state was neither chosen nor anticipated.

Like most of the things we are required to do, living alone takes certain skills. Having lived with someone for years, most of us don't develop those skills. Perhaps the perennial bachelor or spinster might give us a clue. Just as splendid homes are often built on land that normally could not support them— by sinking pilaster supports first—so many people have made good lives for themselves without the conventional supports of marriage and the family. What supports the foundation on which they rest their life? Their interests and their activities, of course! The very same elements on which the quality of our life depends even if we have a marital partner.

Most of us get married and start a family as inevitably as we purchase an automobile at a certain stage of life. But more important than having an automobile is having interesting places to drive it to. Similarly, more important than having a wife or husband is having interesting things to do with her or him. It's easy to get swallowed up in routine and use the vehicle of marriage with no more imagination than is involved in driving to the supermarket and back.

The number, richness, and intensity of our interests are always the major determinants of the quality of life. Marriage serves a great function as a buffer against loneliness, but having someone's help and company doesn't guarantee happiness. The vigorous pursuit of our interests does guarantee a deeper satisfaction.

The intriguing thing about this alternative to marriage is that it frequently increases the cast of characters in our life, so that one may, in fact, wind up less alone than many married people are. The mere physical closeness of people who share little is often not enough to combat loneliness. It's much the same thing as being lonely in a crowd. If the highlights in a couple's life emanate from their TV set rather than from each other, they live on the edge of loneliness. Compare this with someone whose political, musical, and athletic interests involve him five or six nights each week with a variety of people whom he enjoys. Although there are inevitably spaces in his life, he may nonetheless be having more fun than people who live in a family. He may even feel a greater sense of closeness because his ties to others stem from choice rather than obligation.

What about those people who worked hard all their lives—too hard—and somehow never got involved in avocational activities? Is it too late? Of course my answer is a resounding NO. It'll never be earlier! The thing to do *at once* is to look up the most enthusiastic people you know and hitch yourself to their coattails. The point is that it's not so much what they may be interested in as the amount of excitement they stir up. The important thing is to get close to your feelings. Passion over deliberation—that's the order of priorities to begin with. Once you feel strongly about something, you can—believe it or not—feel strongly about other things too. Ordinarily we don't recognize this, because we think logically. But that's not the way we feel! The trick is to come to feel strongly about something, anything, and then other things will happen. You might easily find yourself absorbed in not one but several ideas, causes, interests, or activities. You've struck oil! You're rich! You're no longer dragging your feet. You're alive, energetic. There aren't enough hours in the day. People populate your life. You may occasionally be annoyed and irritated with them—that's part of it all. But you know where you're going. And there are people with you all the way!

Dating Again

Most elderly people we know are married. They enjoy a sense of companionship interrupted only by death or divorce. In recent years, a rise in the number of divorces after many years of marriage has added considerably to the number of older people suffering from a sense of loss and loneliness. This despair is not mitigated by reminding ourselves of the history of a bad marriage. Living for years with someone else, however unhappily, generally predisposes us to a continued need for the presence of another. Although we don't make the transition instantaneously—as do the British when they proclaim, "The King is dead; long live the King"—we must recognize as they do that life goes on. Most people find their lonely state very painful, but they also feel awkward and inept about doing anything about it. In the case of the death of a marital partner, the problem is often even more difficult.

The first obstacle to remove is the guilt generated by a natural desire to be with someone else after the death of a spouse. As we've discussed, the grief of mourning, however deeply and genuinely felt, brings no one back and often hastens the bereaved to his own grave. Our moral obligations are far better served by the good we do a person during his or her life than by the piety we express after a death. Whether we socialized widely or not in the past, and whether beginning to socialize again is easy or not, the fact is that it is necessary.

It's easy to sit around and do nothing when a cold shadow

of despair looms over us. But *doing* something about our plight is the first order of the day. Second, we must recognize the need to persevere. Not all our efforts will be rewarding, and allowing ourselves to be discouraged invites failure. Our efforts must become habitual. Third, it helps to be imaginative in what we do to keep our old friends and to make new ones. Since many of us are not especially strong in this area, let's push ourselves to do something different, something new. Invite a friend or friends to breakfast, to watch an important sports event on TV, or to view a sunrise from a special vantage point. Fourth, recognize that the process of repopulating our world will frequently require spending money. One of the unpleasant realities of life is that so much of it carries a price tag, but let's think of this as an investment that will pay off as our pleasure increases.

As we spend more enjoyable time with people, it's virtually inevitable that we'll begin to see members of the opposite sex. It's probably been so long since we dated, it's understandable that we might initially be unsure of ourselves. What to say, who should make the next move, how much to expect, all make our head spin with doubt and uncertainty. We feel ashamed, at our age, of our own ineptness. We totally overlook the simple fact that the person we're dating is probably in exactly the same position and just as rusty. Additionally, our new role doesn't really call for the sweeping, dramatic gestures of a young Lochinvar. Although a certain amount of charm is always relevant, more often than not what's really needed is simple, unadorned honesty. Why try to be what we're not in the first place? We're seeking friendship, a relationship, not a conquest. It's fine if the relationship grows into something amorous, but there's no reason to feel like a failure if you don't experience spontaneous combustion. Making dates with members of the opposite sex is essentially no different from our general effort to be with people. If we handle dating this way, it will be easier for us to be ourselves, even if we are uncertain and clumsy at times.

An equally important principle to govern our conduct in this matter is that we make sure to date in the plural. Because we're out of practice, we easily overreact when we see only one person with the possibility of romance in mind. We have no basis for comparison, no yardstick, because of our inexperience. It's interesting to notice how many people there are who complain about the lack of freedom in marriage and then bind themselves to a one-to-one relationship soon after they've dissolved a marriage. There are many things to consider before becoming serious—particularly for the elderly. Often a woman will discover that the man she has selected is more her patient than her husband. Or a man may find that his new partner nags and complains about his avocational pursuits no less frequently and vehemently than his wife did.

The most sensible way to think of dating is as a reshuffling of the deck. No matter whom we pick, we cannot expect to play the same hand over, so we may as well mix the cards. Not that we want a totally random hand dealt to us. We want to choose, but first let's find out what's in the deck. Dating will help us see what's there and, more important, help us to understand ourselves more realistically.

Falling in Love Again

Falling in love again, for all its romantic glow, is by no means unusual. It's happening now more than ever. It's not that we're more romantic; it's just that we get divorced so much more often that more of us are footloose and fancy-free. What's more, this is happening at any age. A little over a generation ago, when divorce was first becoming an acceptable reality, it occurred during the third, fourth, and fifth years of marriage or, at the latest, during the ninth and tenth years. Now it takes place any time—even after thirty years of marriage. And the statistics on marrying again remain the same— namely, most people who divorce remarry. What this means is that falling in love again is no longer a thing of youth. It need not be a young romantic who sweeps the object of his affection off on his white steed. Nowadays, there are people in their sixties, seventies, even eighties, who fall in love again.

There are still other changes in society that promote this phenomenon. Not only has our life expectancy been increased, but so has the vigor of age. The redistribution of wealth has helped create a larger class of financially independent elders in our society. Earlier in our history, when a man stopped working for reasons of age and health, he lived not by himself, as he does now, but with one of his children and his family. That was also the common solution for widows. Nothing more was expected of them than to be as little trouble as possible. Their life narrowed, and little thought was given

to starting all over again. One of the benefits of today's loos-
ening of family ties is the freedom many of our elders have
to live their own life.

One of the major interests people now show in their vintage
years is not in just living life out, waiting to die, but in
improving the quality of their remaining years. This alone
accounts for the huge migration to the Sun Belt. In particular,
those who have lost their mate feel the need for replacement.
The strength of this need easily matches that of forty or fifty
years earlier, which generated one's first love. Not that some
of those early needs for sex and possessiveness are not also
present, but the need for companionship and sharing now
become equally demanding. In fact, it can make us as silly
and foolish in our overevaluations as we were forty or fifty
years ago.

Here we should pause. We have little reason to believe
that the first person who comes along is right for us. It's a
simple fact of human nature that the stronger our desire, the
more readily we see what we want to—whether it's really
there or not. We call this autistic or wishful thinking. Actually,
we need a refresher course in going out with the opposite
sex. It's been a long time! There's no reason to believe we
really know how to relate to them, no matter how pleasant
our time with any one of them may be. We can get hurt if
we allow ourselves to fall in love recklessly. Ideally, love is
not a mere sense of elation on the discovery of something;
love is a kind of intimacy of feeling, thought, and desire, and
it takes patient plumbing of the depth and intricacies of our
being before it is truly developed. We have an express ele-
vator to whisk us up to a state of heightened feeling, but
getting down into the nitty-gritty of what each of us is inside
takes a lot more time.

There are more opportunities available today than ever

before to avoid a life of loneliness. Among the elderly, people reach out to each other out of common experience. Friendship on all levels is available, not to mention necessary, for us. Even love is available, but because it requires more of us, it can be costly. It's best to allow it to emerge slowly out of friendship—not with one person but with many.

Remarrying

Marrying again is probably an even better idea than having married the first time. The reason is that having been married makes marriage even more important to us than it seemed when we were single. A bad marriage sours us on our choice, but not on the institution itself. We need each other despite the shortcomings we may find. We are truly social animals and realize our potential best through and with others. We know all this deep down in our bones and, in fact, do remarry following a divorce or death more often than not. By remarrying, will we just make do, make our lives better, or not make it at all? What ought we know to improve our chances?

In the first place, being older (and wiser?) doesn't at all guarantee that we're going to act differently. Having experience and using it are two different things. This is one reason why divorce rates don't improve much in second marriages. Changing a marital partner doesn't guarantee happiness nearly so assuredly as a change in ourselves. The best single change is one that starts with an attitude and ends with doing something about it. The attitude should not be that you've found someone to make you happy. No, it's time to decide that you must make yourself happy and that you've found someone to be happy with you. If you're attracted to your new partner, it should be a pleasure to work on this, and if you've chosen wisely, there will be enough positive feedback to add to your happiness.

Next, it's important for us to approach second and third marriages as different from the first. It's simply unrealistic to believe that we are literally starting all over again. We never do. Of course we get second (and more) chances in life, but we never stay the same. Why should we want what we had ten or twenty or forty years ago? There have been changes in us and in our life situations too. At twenty-two we probably wanted a man or a woman who had eyes only for us; today we want someone who can relate to our grandchildren and enjoy them with us. It's like buying a home in a new climate: the one you lived in up North is hardly appropriate on the edge of a Southern beach. Ideally, a new marriage is as much a blend of life-styles as it is of personalities.

Third, not only are subsequent marriages different from the first, but that difference itself must take on important value. More than we realize, we worship sameness. Without even being aware of it, a man expects to go on just as he had before, the only change in his life being the presence of a new woman. But she is also a *different* woman, probably equally resistant to change. Yet this very difference can generate excitement, interest, and adventure. The whole idea of a new marriage, even if the old one was a good one unfortunately terminated by illness and death, is *not* to pick up where you left off. If you do that, it's not a new marriage at all; it's the same old one, with a partner who is less experienced and good at making it work. The idea is to strike out in new directions, using your new partner's ways and interests as points on the compass.

Marriage is always ideally more than a mere coming together of two individuals. The concept of romantic love has clouded our perceptions of togetherness. It takes much longer than the length of a courtship and wedding ceremony before people are really married. They have a lot to learn from each other and should be willing students. The influence must go both ways. Unless they lend themselves with the necessary effort to the modifications they ask from each other, their relationship will weaken. Their marriage must get better to avoid getting worse, because it simply won't stay the same. It's always this way in an intimate relationship, because so many emotions and thoughts are involved. Intimacy, of course, is the most treasured aspect of a marriage relationship, but it also exposes us and makes our deepest relationship the most fragile. This is why love demands tenderness to stay alive.

Despite the hazards of marriage, Socrates, the wisest of men, enjoined us all to marry. His own marriage, to a most difficult woman by the name of Xantippe, was a disaster. Nonetheless, he suggested that if we chose well, we'd be happy; and if, like him, we chose poorly, then at least we too would become philosophers from the experience.

THERE'S ALWAYS ROOM FOR IMPROVEMENT

As a general psychological principle, it is not advisable to spend too much of our time examining ourselves. This advice is, of course, contrary to today's fashionable opinion, which directs so much attention to us that we virtually become our own patients. We constantly study our own case history and get so wrapped up in ourselves that we soon lose our perspective. It's much like looking at your face in a convex mirror: every pore in your skin assumes the size of a crater on the moon. Once we begin to use such self-magnification, we never finish. It's in our best interest to remain actively involved with others and lose ourselves in the experiences we share with them.

Ironically, it is precisely in others that we will find a solution to the problem of self-examination. It's difficult indeed to be objective about ourselves; the more we look, the more involved and subjective we become. Our major hope lies in being able to see ourselves more clearly through others. It's unfortunate that the mass of psychological information available to us has not at all improved our ability to listen to people. We've become more concerned with ourselves than ever, and we judge people more unhesitatingly than we once did. If only we truly listened to them, we'd hear the small ways their own self-interest colors their reports. We'd hear it again and again, ever more loudly and clearly. If we took one more short step toward objectivity, admitted we're all alike under the skin, we would be forced to see that we, too, have such faults. If we cannot learn from others, we are cheating ourselves out of the richest learning material available.

If we are careful to do it only occasionally, and with the use of others as a mirror, taking inventory of ourselves can be helpful. The more honestly objective we are, the smaller the chance of getting overly involved and making self-examination an end in itself. This chapter is designed to call our attention to some aspects of our behavior that are easily overlooked, especially in our later years. Being age sixty or beyond, we've all had plenty of time to develop habits and settle into routines, and we seldom take time to evaluate their appropriateness or effectiveness: if something's worked for half a century, why think about changing it now? It's true that experience is a good teacher, but only if we learn from it—not if we just live through it. So, without dwelling unhealthily on our problems and worries, and taking advantage of what we can learn from the behavior of others, we can evaluate such things as how successful we really are at making friends, how appropriate our appearance is, how much we talk and how little we may listen, and so on. Particularly at a time in our lives when it's very easy to become set in our ways, it's more important than ever that we remember (to make use of another cliché) that there's always room for improvement. That is, after all, the whole point of this book— and the best attitude to adopt to carry us happily through life.

Living in the Here and Now

In a world that changes as fast as ours does, it's perfectly understandable that we make frequent comparisons between what was and what is. You revisit a city after a couple of years, to find its skyline changed. You run into an associate who tells you about some mutual friends who have gotten divorced. "Why, they were married for over twenty-five years!" you exclaim. "I saw them a year ago and they were getting along as well as ever." The appliances and gadgetry that surround us are constantly being electrified, computerized, miniaturized, and diversified. Manners and styles of dress change so drastically that it becomes hard to tell the good guys from the bad, the rich from the poor, even male from female.

Caught in the maelstrom of such change, we're easily tempted to think better of the past, "the good old days." How often do we hear people make such comments as, "Things sure aren't what they used to be," or, "It wasn't that way when I was a kid"? Generally, there's a shaking of the head to accompany these remarks, suggesting disapproval of the present and a sentimental hankering for our now-distant yesterdays. No doubt we all nurture many sweet memories that add to the enjoyment of life. The trouble is, they are not always reliable, objective, and totally representative. Our memory is highly selective, generally colored, and often even creative. Yes, we're actually capable of fondly remembering things that never happened! It's like Maurice Chevalier singing, "Ah, yes, I remember it well," his desires amply making up for the gaps in his memory.

Far more important than the tricks memory plays on us through its inaccuracies is what it does to our orientation toward life. The here and now—that urgent moment we call the present—is blurred by the mistiness of our dreams of the past. Our adjustment to today is undermined, weakened, by our inattention, distracted by the haunting quality of our sentimental attachment to yesterday. Without realizing it, we have become more and more resistant to accommodating ourselves to today's life. The past tense dominates our speech to a point where not only is the present neglected but the future is almost entirely deprived of its existence. We fall out of step with others younger than we, and we lose the thrust that hope and plans for the future should give us.

Mr. C. is such a person. He happens to be a good storyteller; people start out by liking him, but he wears thin after a while. They get tired of hearing, "That reminds me" (something always reminds him), followed by a tale of twenty or thirty years ago. Discussions of news events or politics always get twisted into declarations of what some former President would have done. Mr. C. gets left out of things because he never seems to want to try anything new. People like him but feel he's not living in their time zone.

More important, Mr. C. has failed himself by not accepting what he *is* rather than what he *was*. Just as we have conveniences today that we didn't in times gone by, such as TV, air conditioning, dishwashers, and calculators, so does he have better judgment and understanding than he once had. Instead of relying so heavily on his memory—which provides little more than a retrospective of his life—using his experience and judgment would enable him to interact more with others, to add to his experience, to involve himself in the present;

in short, to continue to live life instead of just talking about it.

Given a realistic, up-to-date orientation, a person can see more clearly what's better and what's worse in life today compared to yesterday. It is true that many things aren't what they were, but we must realize that not every change represents a decline. Some things get better and some get worse. There's probably a great deal of truth in that old French axiom "The more things change, the more they remain the same." Particularly after sixty, we must accept the here and now and learn to live happily in it.

Self-pity vs. Self-realization

One of the pleasures of being 60+ is having time for people.
No longer do we have to see them on the run. The leisurely
pace of life allows us to sit and talk at will. What can spoil it
for us is that now we seem to hear more complaints than ever
in our conversations. Two of the unquestionable certainties
of life are that no one likes a crybaby and that no one rec-
ognizes that he himself may be one. There's no special problem in figuring out why we dislike people who cry on our
shoulder about their bad luck, their unappreciated virtues,
their innocence and good intentions. Even when we feel sorry
for them, we can't help deploring their lack of maturity. More
often, although we don't express it, we feel that maybe they
were more than a little to blame for what happened to them,
and their chronic ineptness bores us. We don't recognize this
characteristic in ourselves, because we actually believe what
we are saying: "I'm not complaining; I'm reporting the facts!
I really was taken advantage of, misled, promised things that
later weren't delivered."

How can we learn from others unless we see in ourselves
what we see in them, good or bad? The fact is, we *are* like
them: we, too, are complainers and crybabies. The most common mode of adjustment to our problems is not primarily
prevention and cure, as it should be, but some expression of
dismay that we have them at all. "Why does this have to
happen to me?" "There certainly was no earthly reason to

expect that this would take place!" "You have no idea what delay, inconvenience, even suffering was caused by So-and-so's inattention, misrepresentation, dishonesty," etc.

Why do we treat our problems as though talking about them was the only way to deal with them? Why don't we take action, find more effective precautions against getting bilked? Even though we're obviously not in total control, we know that to some degree we make our own luck. Why are so many of us, like an accident-prone person, confronted again and again with the same bad breaks? We've got to be doing something wrong!

But how can we find the answers to these questions when we keep looking in the wrong place? How can we learn to correct our shortcomings when most of our effort goes into feeling sorry for ourselves, blaming others, and justifying our own behavior? Sure, we'd rather be the victor than the victim, but as soon as anything begins to go wrong, we become more concerned with how we feel and look both to ourselves and others than with how we could affect the final result. We continue to hope we'll have our way, but we begin at once to "explain" why we're not getting it. We've taken our eyes off the target, and we're repeating and reinforcing our conviction that the obstacles are too great for us, that we need luck on our side to win. It's more realistic to prepare for trouble than to depend on such a fickle partner as luck.

The decision to be prepared for any outcome is relevant in leisure-time activities such as sports, as well as in the handling of our daily affairs, large or small. The obstacles must be figured in! Those unkind forces of fate are all part of reality. Unless we count on this and prepare accordingly, we will keep getting ambushed, hurt, and discouraged by turns of events familiar enough in our experience for us to have avoided and overcome them. And after surrendering to

obstacles we settle into self-pity. Self-fulfillment and realization become more and more an empty dream.

Granted, it's difficult to change old habits and some, like
the way we interpret things, are so ingrained we hardly see
them. But we can hear ourselves—if we listen, we can hear
our excuses. That's the clue! Whenever we use excuses, we're
talking about our failures rather than trying to avoid them.
Crazily enough, we enjoy this, because we're so self-absorbed.
The tendency for people to beat their breasts in unison is
common enough and easily understandable. They actually
develop a relationship by taking turns "tsking" over each other's woes. It's like a ritual formalizing whining into socially
acceptable behavior. It brings people closer together—but
for the wrong reasons, encouraging crying rather than laughter and making a celebration of weakness and defeat. Nothing
could be further from the goal of self-realization. Why relive
what was unpleasant in the first place? Wisdom dictates the
need for a new game plan to avoid rehashing some unhappy
incident that we should file away until it's truly useful to draw
on that experience again.

Maybe if we talked to others more about *them*selves instead
of *our*selves, about events and activities outside us, we
wouldn't need our excuses. And without excuses, we'd have
a new orientation that might even crowd out the effects of
our failures.

Making Friends after Sixty

Many people grow into their sixties with lots of friends. Even though some old friends may pass on or move to other sections of the country, these people continue to make new friends. It's those who never made many friends earlier in their lives who run into trouble later on. Strange as it sounds, many such people don't realize that they weren't very sociable. Work was such a prevailing factor in their lives that they neglected almost everything else. Their involvement with co-workers and customers was easily mistaken for socializing, and not until they stopped working did they find themselves alone and friendless. Worse yet, they're often without the social skills necessary to make friends. What is someone in this situation to do?

Let's start by underscoring the importance of friendship in our vintage years. We fell into a social life spontaneously during our childhood and teens. In college all we had to do was raise our voice to have company. Many of us continued to cherish and nourish our friendships during our adult life. Others found little time for fun and games (and people). But more than we realize, we became habituated to the inter-action between ourselves and others, whether for business or for pleasure. We were involved with people—even if they annoyed us much of the time. Having been conditioned over the years to being surrounded by people, we're left with a real need for them. Just as we stay trim and maintain our body tone by exercise, so we can maintain the tone of our emotional life by interaction. You can jog alone; but interaction requires others.

It's easy enough to recognize this—the difficulty is in doing something about it. We've all heard about the man who says, "Every time I feel like doing some exercise, I lie around and wait until the feeling goes away." There are also people who say: "It's not that I don't want to make friends; it's just that everyone I meet is such a complainer and a bore." Maybe, but maybe this is just sour grapes. Worse yet, maybe this is a self-portrait! Perhaps it's you who are boring.

To a fairly large degree, people are what we elicit from them. How interesting and enthusiastic have you been in the company of others? Have you been a genuinely good listener? Do you draw out the best in someone you meet, or do you passively let him ramble on about matters that don't interest you? Listening and eliciting conversation are the skills which help make interaction outside of business more satisfying. Needless to say, we can't wish them into existence. The effective alternative is to go about it the same way you would learn to sail or improve your game of golf, only without a teacher. That makes it a real challenge, doesn't it?

I believe I can reduce the enormity of the job with a few suggestions to get you started. First, make a deal with yourself that you will not make a single critical comment until you've met thirty new people, and seen a dozen of them at least once again. Second, make arrangements to meet again right then and there. Third, practice listening. Don't just listen passively—ask questions. You'll know how well you did by how much you can tell your spouse later about your new friend.

Notice the exclusion so far of any reference to what you like or dislike in people. All that comes later. Like a baseball player, you'll swing at a lot of bad pitches before you learn to save yourself for the good ones. But that's how you learn—really learn. Later on, you'll go still further in your relationships with people. For example, you'll become skillful at minimizing the use of the past tense—by them and by yourself.

None of this will happen overnight, of course. More than we realize, we're all victims of our own bad habits. Often we have a tendency to blow our own horn, complain too much, not smile enough, or show no interest, enthusiasm, or willingness to try something new. Strange that when we have nothing to sell but ourselves we don't put our best foot forward. Also, we're all a little spoiled by our previous relationships. After all, those that stuck came out of serious searching, and now we have to do that all over again.

Let's get to the icing on the cake. The best part of making friends after sixty is the huge variety open to us. Earlier in our lives, most of us were more clannish than we realized. We sought out and selected none but kindred spirits—people in the same neighborhood or school, in the same or related business, of the same socioeconomic status. We were birds of a feather. Now that we're freer, let's use that freedom and explore differences, rather than withdraw from them. You can turn your auto mechanic, your hardware-store man, your butcher, or the local policeman into a friend. Invite him to lunch, for a drink, or to go fishing with you. Most important of all, *get to know young people!* There's no better way to remain "young." The energy you gain will be reflected in your language, your awareness of issues, your humor, and, most important, in a sense of liveliness and youth. The way to go about this is to meet your friends' children: get to know them, invite them to the theater with you, take them out on your boat with their friends, do things for them. If your tennis is good enough, play with them. Teach your friend's daughter macrame. The list is endless.

There's a great deal of value in what we have to give and in what we receive from others. In a way, we tend to act like sleeping giants, failing to fulfill our potential. With a little application we can all develop the habit of continually renewing our social life. We must not let ourselves rest on our laurels and remain satisfied with the friendships we have. We will stay young by doing what we did when we *were* young, and one of those things was to make friends. We now have more experience to bring to our relationships, and in so doing, we will find the bonus of replenishing ourselves.

Talking and Listening

Talking and listening are, of course, two of the major ingredients of social life. We open our hearts and our minds by sharing with each other what we feel and think, what experiences we've had, what plans, hopes, and desires occupy us. But many of us, frankly, talk too much and listen poorly. Others are too often silent. It's not easy to develop the right balance. The good conversationalist is not simply a good storyteller, who may be highly entertaining, even spellbinding, but could be very poor at bringing someone else out. He may not even give anyone else a chance. The person who knows how to talk *and* listen is the one who invites participation.

The reason for considering the issue of how much we talk and how much we listen is that the lifelong difficulty we have in maintaining a proper balance is almost always increased with age. Many of us get tired and easily go to one or the other extreme—we only half listen, if that, and nod our head and grunt; or having accumulated so many experiences, we become dramatic in describing them and talk non-stop. Everything and anything reminds us of a story that we must tell, leaving no time to listen. Age doesn't affect all of us the same way, but there's one thing we can be certain of: whatever it is that we were, we'll get to be more so. There are many reasons—not very good, but compelling nonetheless—why most of us prefer talking to listening. In our anxiety to make a good impression, we tend to say things that will bring attention to the virtues we want people to see in us—how funny we are or how successful or what important people we know, etc. Additionally, we are fed so many TV talk shows on which nobody seems to take the time to think. Talk is the important thing. And maybe, because we cannot participate and answer TV talk, we do all our listening there and make up for lost chances to talk in live situations. But there's an important lesson here. We do, in fact, learn a lot from TV conversations *because* we listen. We don't learn much when we do most of the talking.

Luckily, we're not chained forever to what we were or to what we are. If we sharpen our awareness of why it's good for us to talk but equally good for us to listen, the chances are we can make a better mix of them, so that they will both work for us. We must keep in mind that just as friendliness demands that certain human sounds emanate from us in the direction of someone else, it also asks that we listen to the sounds approaching us with enough attention and interest to respond. This may be simplistic, but how many times after you've left someone can you remember anything he has asked or said? You either monopolized the "conversation" or never elicited anything from your partner. He may have been dull, but if you're willing to believe, as I do, that you can learn something from everyone, then you failed; you didn't give him a chance.

A good rule of thumb to apply to your speech is the architectural reminder that "less is more." Trim the fat, cut it down. (Lincoln's Gettysburg Address, as well as scores of other famous historical messages, took no more than several minutes.) We must free ourselves from addiction to detail. Give your listener a chance to figure things out, to understand, to ask questions. If you tell him everything and he doesn't have to think, his listening will take so little effort that he'll become inattentive and bored.

One of the major threats of age is that it can bring increased isolation. Friends die, co-workers no longer surround us after retirement; we even start life in a new place, knowing no one. If we want to fill our social needs, we must develop our conversational skills. This consists of learning how to talk *and* how to listen. Make questions an important part of your dialogue. Skip details until someone asks about them. Don't try to make your big impression right off. Listen and learn; let others find out who and what you are. They'll wind up liking you more for it, and you'll feel the same about them.

Fitting Appearance to Self-image

Surely no one doubts the fact that we live in a world of glittering appearance. The underlying reality is always skillfully dressed to look better than it is. If philosophers have ruminated with only marginal success over the problems of separating appearance and reality, we common folk don't have a chance. We're inundated by the extravagant language of advertising, with its hyperbole and high-pressure sales promotion. Packaging is made equally compelling and frequently involves more design, ingenuity, and cost than the thing packaged. It's very hard—almost impossible—to remain untouched by so pervasive an influence. Before long, we become more accepting of fads and fashions than we realize. Our choices are more often made for us than by us. It's too hard to fight, and except for critical exceptions, it's not worth it. The bottom line is that our economy has made appearance important, and there's every indication that our society is going to remain appearance-oriented.

In addition to the fact that big business exploits appearance is the even more significant one that we ourselves can't help stressing its importance. How else do we judge people except in terms of what they put in evidence? Would you feel comfortable about a new neighbor who appeared unkempt and unshaven? (You may learn later that he's a Nobel Prize-winning physicist.) Would a bank hire a highly qualified young man with a ponytail? Don't we all dress for the occasion when

we deem it appropriate? It's essentially in our own best interest to put our best foot forward. Rightly or wrongly, we
are judged by our appearance, just as we judge others by
theirs. Perhaps even more important, our feelings about ourselves are also influenced by how we think we look. In other
words, we too judge ourselves (if not totally at least partially)
by appearance. Granted, we seem to have different eyes and
mirrors when we look at ourselves, but despite our subjec-
tivity, there's a lot we can't help seeing.

It doesn't help us to feel good about ourselves if we're fatter
than we want to be. If we don garments that show no attention
to taste or appropriateness and seem to be a "uniform" for
the elderly, we can't expect people to treat us as equals.
Anyone is bound to wonder about his acceptability once he
learns his breath smells. And so on. We must be sensitive to
such lapses and look at improving our appearance as a big
trade-off—we have to *give* something for everything we *get*.
We will lose weight by giving up the delights of snacks and
overeating. We'll improve our looks by carefully choosing
flattering outfits. We'll get rid of bad breath by giving our
gums the appropriate care.

Unfortunately, many elderly people devote their lives to
sitting around, essentially waiting to die. Old age becomes a
period in which they give up, stop caring for themselves and
the world, let themselves go. Illness becomes the only source
of drama in their lives. But keeping up appearances is worthwhile; it really pays off. By strenuously maintaining the
impression we make on others, we can keep in better shape
for ourselves too. We can't help but feel pleased when we
get favorable reactions from people.

Our relationships to people are of the first order of importance. How we conduct them can make or break our vintage years. In order to learn to increase our appeal to others,

we need to recognize what we like in them. Isn't it time we opened ourselves to their vitality and tried to imitate it? They're not talking about their illnesses all the time. So-and-so often has a joke—good. Another friend can always be counted on to try something new. Don't you quietly envy the way someone else looks—his hair is nicely coiffed, he doesn't have landscape plantings growing out of his nostrils and ears, he doesn't scrape along in old man's shoes. Still another acquaintance is always willing to help.

It's worth working to meet the challenge of imitating those things we like in others. The effort is good for us. Unlike the philosophers who struggle to distinguish appearance from reality, we can enjoy turning our appearance into an honest and impressive reflection of what we really are inside.

Eat Less, Drink Less, and Be Merry

Years ago, people who lived by the saying "Eat, drink, and be merry" were said to have achieved the good life. Today, our increased understanding of the requirements of good health tempers that attitude. Although we do not deny the pleasures of good food and drink, we question dependence on them. The sophisticated suggestion is made that such dependence may even imply a lack of satisfaction of emotional needs. Excess indulgence, in particular, signals not merriment so much as anguish, conflict, and unhappiness. This is a far cry from the old, simple belief that an overweight or a drunk person was a happy one. There's much evidence nowadays supporting moderation in eating and drinking, and the clear implication is that we should find our merriment elsewhere.

But do we take heed? Do we act on what we know? Fast-food places have proliferated around us in such huge numbers that we almost constantly face the temptation of a hamburger, a hot dog, pizza, fried chicken, or an ice-cream cone. Not to mention the vast emporiums, called supermarkets, with mountainous supplies of food available, in many instances twenty-four hours a day. Even our own homes become storage places complete with oversized refrigerators, freezers, and pantries. We never seem to be more than a few steps away from food. If we are, it's brought to us, as in sports arenas, theaters, and parks. Living in a modern community means being near restaurants and other people's homes, where we can also eat. Friendship is most often expressed by allowing ourselves to be stuffed by our friends' caloric hospitality. In the face of all this, it's certainly not easy to practice moderation.

We're also victims of our own bad habits. If we feel a little sorry for ourselves, we have an extra-special snack. If we're frustrated and angry, we eat more. If we're bored, we scavenge about for something to eat. If we can't sleep, we raid the refrigerator. It sometimes reaches a point where no matter what we feel, we're ready to eat. Why? Because eating is a source of satisfaction! We don't eat because we're hungry— we rarely wait for that. We eat out of habit, routine, and the desire for gratification. Our needs for love, admiration, recognition, achievement, are often blocked and left painfully unfulfilled. Food is, in our affluent world, always nearby, and eating thus becomes our most convenient source of gratification.

The trouble is, of course, that we get fat. As a friend of mine puts it, "Everything I eat goes to my stomach." Especially as we age, overeating makes our midsection get heavier and our legs, out of lack of exercise, skinnier. Even walking becomes more of an effort; our breath comes in short pants, and most serious of all, our heart has to strain to perform its normal, everyday jobs. In short, we're paying dearly for the pleasure of self-indulgence. We are unquestionably shortening our life, as well as turning our body into a burden. It's no longer the pleasure it once was to use it in athletics, or even in the more prosaic pursuits of everyday life, such as bending, stretching, lifting, and walking.

The good cheer so often expressed in drinking with friends exposes us to similar risks. Alcohol is fattening and, of course, habit-forming. It's easy for the drinking to spread from cocktail time to other, not so cheerful times. And the more it does, the less cheering alcohol becomes. Time, once one of our major assets, is transformed into vacuous, unproductive periods, with nothing to show for them but a hangover and an ever-deepening sense of worthlessness and guilt.

The answer to our potential excesses in eating and drinking is not in pious, well-intentioned promises—always made after an indulgence. We would do just as well to promise ourselves to be happy, because if we were, we wouldn't be substituting these easily available sources of satisfaction for the real thing. But what is the real thing? What truly makes us happy? Most people immediately think of being rich, famous, healthy, free, more talented, but we can have any and all of these and still feel miserable. Only one thing is really certain: most of us *don't* have all these assets. So the question must really be restated: can't we find ways to be happy with what we *haven't got*?

If we looked at it this way, we'd be less given to frustration and disappointment. We would not be driven to settle for superficial satisfactions simply because of their availability, with no regard for the risks they entail. In settling for less, we'd get more. We could eat less, drink less, and be merry.

The Habit of Laughter

Why do we laugh when someone slips on a banana peel—a potentially painful event? Why does Charlie Chaplin, cold and hungry, amuse us by eating a pair of old shoes? Sad situations are turned into rollicking comedy mainly because, to put it simply, if we didn't laugh we'd cry. Psychologists have come to see laughter as a method of unconsciously protecting ourselves from feeling brokenhearted over a sad predicament. There are serious philosophers—existentialists, to be specific—who urge us to recognize that much of the suffering and inequity in life is absurd, ridiculous. But it's hard to see the humor in anything close to us because of our habitual overreaction to pain, deprivation, or insult. Our total attention is easily absorbed by anything that hurts. We lose our sense of proportion, our perspective, our evaluation of the relative importance of things around us. Our responsiveness may increase, but we become overly responsive to the wrong things. A person with such an oppressive outlook hardly ever laughs, and finds nothing ridiculous. There is never any relief in sight for him.

I do not mean to claim that there is no tragedy, pain, or suffering in life. But even while there is ugliness and sadness, who can deny that beauty and humor also abound in life? It's all there; what we find depends on our temperament and training. Some people can see the humor in a situation more easily than others. They're not necessarily better educated, richer, or wiser, nor are they professional comedians (who, incidentally, are more often than not fairly humorless about themselves). They are people like you or me who, fortunately, over the years have developed *the habit of laughter*.

Is it too late, deep into adulthood, to develop the habit of laughter? I think not. The easiest way is to expose yourself to it. It's like learning a foreign language by living with the people who speak it, rather than by taking courses. In a sense, learning to see the humor in things is changing our mode of expression. We look up, not down; we let things glance off us instead of knocking us over. Being with people who can laugh helps, but we've got to encourage them with appropriate responses. This means smiling, even if at times we don't think they're funny.

Second, we've got to push ourselves into a search for humor. Like bird-watchers who go out to the woods with binoculars, we cannot expect it all to come to us. Stop in the stationery store you often pass and read the amusing greeting cards. Don't settle for "I can never remember a joke." Remember it! And tell it! It gives you a chance to laugh all over again. Select funny things to read. Get people to tell you the amusing incidents in their life—who wants to hear about their illnesses?

Once we begin to laugh more often, we begin to feel differently about things; we see them differently. It's always this way. Psychologists have come to recognize that if we change our behavior, our feelings will follow. Most people think it's the other way around, but they've been proved wrong. How can we make anyone feel differently about some upsetting experience unless we first distract him and make him laugh? The truth is that once we learn to laugh often enough, things are not nearly so upsetting. It's not the joke itself that's at the heart of humor; it's our willingness to lend ourselves to recognizing the element of humor in the event. And this very ability to see what is silly even in a serious situation means that we are aware of all sides of that situation—we are maintaining our healthy perspective, our sense of balance.

The benefits are enormous. For one thing, we can enjoy a lighter step in life. Not everything need be serious. Lightening up is especially valuable in today's world, in which some people have abandoned good humor for abrasive self-assertiveness. Certainly we're better off being amused than annoyed by a pushy person. We keep our blood pressure down while theirs goes up. Instead of suffering from the sad realization that we cannot change the world, we've improved our adjustment to it by learning to perceive and react to it differently. We've cultivated the habit of laughter, and it will see us through.

How Am I Doing Now?

We all have things to worry about, we all have aches and pains, but we all also have things we enjoy a good deal. It can be helpful to take an unbiased look at ourselves—not for the purpose of discovering more to regret or to gloat over, but rather to remind ourselves of what more we can do to improve the quality of our life. For this purpose, I have prepared a series of questions that might help direct your attention to the areas of daily life critically related to its quality. Life is good if we can honestly answer these questions with a resounding "Yes." Even a hesitant "Yes, I think so" to most of the questions is a good sign.

We may ask ourselves:

1. *Do you laugh every day?* This is such a simple matter that we tend to overlook it. But life is sad without it. To paraphrase what the French say about wine, a day without laughter is a day without sunshine. As we've discussed, laughter is a good habit to develop and it's easy to find. The more you laugh, the more easily will you begin to see the humor in everything around you.

2. *Do you see friends or co-workers you like to be with every day?* Or almost every day? Unless a person is enormously creative, being alone is hard. We don't laugh alone. Whatever hurts, hurts more in solitude. Socialize by habit and remember that a successful outcome is as much dependent on you as on others.

3. *Is the time you spend with your spouse enjoyable?* Even if there is a history of conflict, you can still turn a meal together or a TV program you both watch into a pleasant time. It is you who can cause or allow an unpleasant confrontation, and it is you who can turn the tables and create some shared fun.

4. *Do you spend some time each week in physical activity?* Athletics, gardening, even just plain walking, are not only good but essential. Inactivity breeds loss of muscle tone and depression.

5. *Do you have plans, something to look forward to in the future?* We all have a past; the present occupies us momentarily, but it's the future that keeps the bright colors of life gleaming. Make things happen next year by planning them now.

6. *Do you enjoy many of your meals?* Eating can and should be fun. This does not mean we should overeat; we should concentrate on enjoying the whole experience—the people, the place, the conversation.

7. *Do you sleep well?* Sleep is a habit easy to get out of by doing the wrong things, such as choosing the wrong hour, the wrong activities before bedtime, or becoming dependent on pills. Take a look at your habits and change them if that's indicated.

8. *Do you maintain an interest in sex?* It's easy in these days of relative freedom from censorship. Sex needn't be the robust activity of your twenties to be enjoyable—even one piece of pie is better than none.

9. *Do you do something different or new from time to time?* There is hardly anything that matches novelty for sheer revitalizing power. Most of our lives contain more elements of repetition than is good for us. This leads to boredom and a

loss of sensibility. Try something different. Open yourself to the opportunities for it. You'll feel more alive.

10. *Is your life free of clutter?* This question refers to the small details of life, which have a way of building mounds of irritants on your desk, stuffing your drawers, piquing your conscience, and generally weighing you down. It's usually better to be brashly delinquent and use the wastepaper basket. Best of all is to develop the habit of taking care of things when they first come to your attention. The subsequent sense of freedom is worth the initial effort.

It goes without saying that there are many special circumstances in the lives of all of us. And there are forces over which we have little or no control. As we age, it is especially easy for us to feel that these forces are closing in on us. That's why it becomes especially important that we recognize and take advantage of the things we can control. There are quite a few! Work on these. The rewards will be rich.

SUMMING UP

We spend the first twenty-odd years of our life impatiently waiting to be older. We believe being grown up will mean being free. We'll be able to go to sleep when we feel like it and buy what we want; we won't be burdened with homework or with the restrictions and reprimands of parents. But when we reach adulthood, we find the reality is that we must spend most of our waking hours working. Before long, we become saddled with the responsibilities of family life. Still, we seem to derive enough satisfaction to make us hate reaching thirty, dread forty, and regard fifty as the beginning of the end of life. Our initial impatience to grow has changed. After a while, we even feel alarmed—as though we were desperately trying to use unresponsive brakes to halt a vehicle charging down-hill.

Is what lies ahead really so scary? Even though disease and accident can claim people at any age, the statistics are all in our favor—and that's downright realistically comforting. But what bothers most of us more intensely than how long we will live is how "alive" we will be when we do get old. Too often we see in the aged a loss of beauty, strength, and vigor. We see deterioration rather than growth, nostalgia in place of anticipation, monotony instead of variety, endings rather than beginnings. Other older people, however, embrace life with such a great appetite that the habits they develop give them a strong potential for survival. This is not to say that they necessarily live longer, but that they continue to live very full lives to the end. Many of these people do live longer, in fact, because their health is not threatened by a surrender to the adversities of age. Their love of life helps them weather the storms; their habit of enjoyment keeps them from depression and self-pity. The end of life is often as glorious for them as the end of a symphony—a *gran tutti* in which *all* instruments are heard. Taking the same attitude, we can employ all our instruments—or resources—to fill life with satisfaction.

It's of great advantage to develop the habit of living this way as early as possible. It will never be earlier than this moment to start—whether we're thirty-five or sixty-five years old. There are countless interests and activities available to the aged, most of which are the same as those we might have pursued when we were young. We just never took advantage of them. Activity and interests are the ingredients of a good life. Watching TV and thinking only about yourself form the unhealthy diet of those unhappy 60+ers who have given up. The person who truly loves things outside himself—people, activities, ideas, interests—keeps moving. He remains active and alive to the end, because novelty, beginnings, promise, and growth are constantly stirred up by his movement.

The point of *60 +: Planning It, Living It, Loving It* is that a happy life after sixty is more a product of *attitude* than of opportunity and luck. Certainly the latter are important, but like many gifts, they often remain unused. How is the right attitude developed? Not by awaiting some dramatic insight that splits open the heavens, but by getting out and *doing* things, by forcing yourself. We've got to sample activities and do our best to meet new people. Don't say no to any invitation. We have every reason to believe the French when they say, "Appetite comes from eating." In other words, our positive attitude, our zest or appetite for life after sixty will come from *doing*. Facing old age takes courage and perseverance, but it is rising to that challenge that constantly hones our appetite, making us hungry for life. As Cervantes put it, "The best sauce in the world is hunger." It is my earnest hope that the contents of this book have whet the appetites of more than a few 60 + ers.